T0365677

"Linda Clark loves the Lord and wants you to love Him too. *My High Places* bursts with the truth about God's glory and majesty. Read it with a heart of worship!" — Dr. Jordan Stone, Senior Pastor of Redeemer PCA in McKinney, TX and Associate Professor at Reformed Theological Seminary, Dallas.

Linda loves the Word of God. She has faithfully and enthusiastically led biblically sound, engaging, women's Bible studies for more than thirty-five years. Therefore, when she told me she was texting daily devotions to her children and grandchildren, I asked to be put on the list. I looked forward to reading Linda's devotional text message every morning and sharing it with my family. What a blessing it has been! I look forward to using *My High Places* personally and highly recommend it. Mrs. Nancy Kerr, Former VP Marketing, Ligonier Ministries, Lake Mary, FL

MY
HIGH
PLACES

❖

DEVOTIONS FOR SPIRITUAL GROWTH

Linda McGregor Clark

WESTBOW
PRESS®
A DIVISION OF THOMAS NELSON
& ZONDERVAN

This book is a work of non-fiction. Unless otherwise noted, the author
and the publisher make no explicit guarantees as to the accuracy of
the information contained in this book and in some cases, names
of people and places have been altered to protect their privacy.

WestBow Press books may be ordered through booksellers or by contacting:

WestBow Press
A Division of Thomas Nelson & Zondervan
1663 Liberty Drive
Bloomington, IN 47403
www.westbowpress.com
844-714-3454

ISBN: 978-1-6642-0858-2 (sc)
ISBN: 978-1-6642-0859-9 (e)

Print information available on the last page.

WestBow Press rev. date: 10/29/2020

This book is dedicated to my very dear husband of 56 years, Buck Clark. Without his loving encouragement, I would not have put this book together! Thank you, my Love!

INTRODUCTION

There are devotional books by the hundreds and they are written by some really big names, so why in the world would I write another Devotional book, was the question I was asking myself! But after much urging from my husband and a discussion with our Pastor, who said this could be a legacy for me to leave for my Grandchildren and Great Grandchildren, and it occurred to me to be a good way to save all the texts I have been sending to my grandchildren for the last several years. So because I wanted to be able to keep these special truths in front of them when I am gone, I decided to put _My High Places_ together in book form, in order that after I am gone, they will be able at any time to pick up this little book and go through my texts to be reminded of all God's truths I sent them through the years and of how much I loved them and prayed for them.

The story about my text message Devotionals came about as my grandchildren were getting older and of course, each had a phone. As I prayed about staying in touch with them, it seemed to be a good idea for me to use their phones to stay close and why not put a scripture and a prayer in each text, in order that they could learn how to use scripture in their prayers. So, I began. As time has gone by, I have added others to my text group: my children and their spouses, my siblings, my special friends, some of my brothers and sisters from church and their children. My little group has gotten larger!

God, the Lord, is my strength; he makes my feet like the deer's; he makes me tread on my high places. (Habakkuk 3:19 ESV)

God is using my experience of serving and loving my group of readers, to grow my knowledge of Him and to show me more of His love for me and for them. He is making me tread on _MY HIGH PLACES_. One of these days all of us will be called to even higher places. Where all will be gathered to praise our God on the hill of the Lord. My prayer for my grandchildren and any other readers of this book is that God will make you learn to tread on your high places too.

Linda McGregor Clark

GOD'S WORD

━━━━━━━━━━━━━━ ✣ ━━━━━━━━━━━━━━

This statement, which I copied off Twitter, is by one of my favorite Theologians:

> *There are moments when I am so amazed by the holiness of God that I wonder why He permits these sinful hands of mine ever to touch the pages of His holy Word.* **Darrell B. Harrison**

When I read this, I became aware many of us Christians do not have that kind of love for God's Word. So, I decided we need to look at some scripture verses that tell us exactly what God's Word is and what God wants us to do with His Word.

For the word of God is living and active and sharper than any two-edged sword and piercing as far as the division of soul and spirit, and able to judge the thoughts and intentions of the heart. (Hebrews 4:12 NASB)

GOD'S WORD:

1. Living and active
2. Able to judge the thoughts and intentions of our hearts
3. Goes forth from God's mouth
4. Accomplishes what God desires

Holy Spirit as our Teacher open our hearts to understand the importance of reading the Bible, God's Truth. Help the verses we will be reading to change any wrong ideas we have about God's Word and fill us with right intentions and love for God's Word. According to God's Word, may it be so.

All Scripture is given by inspiration of God, and is profitable for doctrine, for reproof, for correction, for instruction in righteousness. (II Timothy 3:16 NKJV)

GOD'S WORD:

1. Came by inspiration of God, which means God breathed
2. Useful to:

   a. Teach what is true
   b. Teach us what is wrong
   c. Teach us to do what's right

3. God uses it to prepare and equip His people to do good work.

O Father, You have given Your Words to chosen men, so they could write the scriptures exactly as if You had written them Yourself. Give us the ability to use Your Word to recognize truth, to understand the wrong we've done and to do what pleases You. In Jesus Christ name So Be It.

LINDA MCGREGOR CLARK

The grass withers, the flower fades, But the word of our God stands forever." (Isaiah 40:8 NKJV)

THOUGHTS:

In this verse, we see that God's Word stands forever. Nothing in God's word ever changes, we can completely trust the Bible because it is God's actual words. I read somewhere the comment that if a person wants to hear God speak, then all he must do is read the Bible out loud. I agree!

Heavenly Father, Your Word is eternal in heaven and on earth. It never changes and is always true. Help us to hold tight to It and to use it as our guide to know You better and to teach us how to live to please You. May it be so.

This is why we constantly thank God, because when you received the word of God that you heard from us, you welcomed it not as a human message, but as it truly is, the word of God, which also works effectively in you who believe. (1 Thessalonians 2:13 CSB)

THOUGHTS:

The Word of God is taught by humans but is truly the Word of God and works effectively in our lives. Therefore, accept the word, which is able to save us, and in humility obey it.

Dear Father God make our hearts willing to follow Your commandments and to be doers of Your word and not just listeners. Asking in Christ Jesus name, may it be so.

So we have the prophetic word confirmed,Know this that no prophecy of Scripture is of any private interpretation, for prophecy never came by the will of man, but holy men of God spoke as they were moved by the Holy Spirit. (II Peter 1:19-21 NKJV)

GOD'S WORD:

1. Prophetic word is another term for the Word of God or Scripture.
2. Not one word of Scripture comes from ideas of men or from their own interpretations.
3. Holy men of God, led by the Holy Spirit, spoke God's word that we have today.

O Father, what a wonderful thing to know that our Bibles are actually Your words to us, so we can believe the truth about Jesus and receive eternal life. Thank You, thank You for the light to shine in this dark world, in Jesus name Amen

LINDA MCGREGOR CLARK

Let the word of Christ dwell in you richly, teaching and admonishing one another in all wisdom. (Colossians 3:16 ESV)

GOD'S WORD:

1. Word of Christ is the Scriptures.
2. Dwell richly means we are so full of the scriptures that our entire life is affected.
3. Admonishing is rebuke, urge, advise
4. Teaching in wisdom

Heavenly Father, we are a long way from having Your holy words dwelling in us richly, it is more like poorly. Forgive us for not loving the word of Christ and make us willing to accept this rebuke and to learn to love the Bible and then give us hearts full of thankfulness. In Jesus Christ name Amen

For whatever was written in earlier times was written for our instruction, so that through endurance and the encouragement of the scriptures we might have hope and overflow with confidence in His promises. (Romans 15:4 AMP)

THOUGHTS:

God's word was written to teach us about not giving up when things get difficult and how to have hope because the Word is absolute Truth and can be trusted completely.

Father, we're going through a very difficult time in our world and all the news is about the danger lurking. We're seeing fear in action all around us and it's hard to hold on to the truth that Your children are in Your hands and nothing can snatch us out of Your hands. Fill us with hope because of Jesus and Your Truth, So Be It.

The law of the Lord is perfect, refreshing the soul. The statutes of the Lord are trustworthy, making wise the simple. The precepts of the Lord are right, giving joy to the heart. The commands of the Lord are radiant, giving light to the eyes. The decrees of the Lord are firm, and all of them are righteous. By them your servant is warned; in keeping them there is great reward. (Psalms 19:7-11 NIV)

GOD'S WORD:

1. Law is perfect and refreshing of the soul
2. Statues are trustworthy and make the inexperienced wise
3. Precepts are right and make hearts glad
4. Commands are radiant and make eyes see the Light (Jesus is the Light of the world)
5. Decrees are reliable and Righteous
6. Gives warnings
7. Obedience means great reward

THOUGHTS:

Fear of the Lord is a good thing, and it comes from reading God's word, and getting to know God well, and then your fear (deep awe) of God will cause you to trust Him and His Word.

O Father what wonderful descriptions of Your Holy Bible and to think You picked out special men to write all these holy words, Your words, for Your children. So that we could know You, learn to fear You, and understand Your wrath over, sin but also Your love of us exhibited in Christ Jesus our Lord. Fill us with love for the Word and a deep desire to grow in obedience to it. In Jesus Christ name Amen

My child, pay attention to what I say; turn your ear to my words, for they are life to those who find them. (Proverbs 4:20-23 NIV)

THOUGHTS:

God's Words have life in them and we must pay attention to them.

O Father give us ears that pay attention to Your Word and hearts to trust in Your words and grow in wisdom. Fill us with the peace of God, which will guard our hearts and our minds. Then the Holy Spirit will help us to be able to guard our hearts and be obedient children. According to Your Word So Be It.

For I am not ashamed of this Good News about Christ. It is the power of God at work, saving everyone who believes. (Romans 1:16 NLT)

GOD'S WORD:

1. Good News about Christ is also called the Gospel and is in the Bible (God's Word)
2. Power of God to save all who believe
3. Tells us how to be right with God through faith in Jesus

GOD'S CHILDREN:

1. Are not ashamed of the Gospel
2. Have faith in the Gospel
3. Are Righteous (repented, are forgiven and are right in God's eyes)
4. Do the work of God by believing in Jesus whom God sent

Give us grace, Heavenly Father, to be faithful, unmoving and unashamed of Jesus in this world that hates Him so much. Build up our faith so that we shine the Light of Jesus everywhere we go. Asking in the Name of our Savior and according to Your Word So Be It.

This is Jesus speaking:

For truly, I say to you, until heaven and earth pass away, not an iota, not a dot, will pass from the Law until all is accomplished. Therefore, whoever relaxes one of the least of these commandments and teaches others to do the same will be called least in the kingdom of heaven, but whoever does them and teaches them will be called great in the kingdom of heaven. (Matthew 5:17-19 ESV)

GOD'S WORD, WHAT ARE WE TO DO WITH IT?:

1. Never add to His Commandments
2. Never take away from God's Word
3. Keep the commandments
4. Jesus did not abolish the Law, but He fulfilled it
5. Know it will last till Heaven and earth die without any changes
6. Do not refuse to obey any of God's commandments or teach others to do so
7. Obey God's commandments and teach others to obey them also

Holy Holy Holy is Your Word, Oh Father help us understand clearly that You have established the Bible, which is Your Word and we are to obey every law, every command, every precept, everything in the Bible without picking and choosing the verses we like or the ones we don't like. The Bible is Your very word from You to Your church and we are to keep and obey it. Please Forgive us when we ignore Your Word,or are disobedient or want to change it or relax it. In Jesus Christ name So Be It

LINDA MCGREGOR CLARK

Forever, O Lord, your word is firmly fixed in the heavens. I will never forget your precepts, for by them you have given me life. (Psalms 119:89,93 ESV)

GOD'S WORD:

1. Is forever fixed (will not change)
2. Gives us life

Such wonderful truths Dear Father! Please give us ears to hear and hearts to believe these statements from the Bible concerning the preciousness of Your Word. Help us to believe and know it never changes, that it is perfect and true and gives us life through Jesus. Fill us with love for You and Your Holy Word, in Jesus's name So Be It.

The mouth of the righteous utters wisdom, and his tongue speaks justice. The law of his God is in his heart; his steps do not slip. (Psalms 37:30-31 ESV)

The person who is righteous is the one who has faith in Jesus and obeys God's Word by:

1. Giving wise counsel
2. Teaching right from wrong
3. Having God's law in their hearts, so they will keep on God's narrow path without slipping.

Heavenly Father, this definition of the righteous person shows us what God's children will be as we grow in our faith. But O God, we have a long way to grow! Thank You that we are righteous in Your eyes as soon as we become Your child, but then we begin to grow in wisdom from above as the Holy Spirit guides us by Your Word. So now as we read Your Word, plant it in our hearts and bring it to our remembrance whenever it will keep us from slipping into sin. In Jesus Christ's, our Lord and Savior, name So Be It.

LINDA MCGREGOR CLARK

This is the one to whom I will look: he who is humble and contrite in spirit and trembles at my word. (Isaiah 66:2 ESV)

THOUGHTS:

God is Creator of all things and nothing exists that He did not make and this omnipotent (all powerful), omnipresent (exists everywhere), omniscient (all knowing) God cares about His children who are humble, repentant and want to obey His Word.

O LORD, this world in which we live is constantly saying Your Holy Word is old fashioned and not really Your actual words. But every verse we've been reading these last two weeks says it is Your Word and we should tremble at it and obey it. Help us understand what it means to be humble toward You, then help us to repent. Asking in Jesus Christ name So Be It.

My word, I send it out, and it always produces fruit. It will accomplish all I want it to, and it will prosper everywhere I send it. (Isaiah 55:10-11 NLT)

GOD'S WORD:

1. Sent out by God
2. Produces fruit
3. Accomplishes what God wants
4. Prospers everywhere God sends it

Blessed are You O Lord for sending out Your Word, give us good soil in our hearts to produce the fruit of belief and understanding and to prosper in our lives for You. Lord God forgive us for letting weeds of sin grow in our hearts. Then dear Holy Spirit reveal to each of us what these sins are, so we can ask for Your help and turn away from them. Asking in the name of Jesus, our Savior and Lord, may it be so.

LINDA MCGREGOR CLARK

This is Jesus praying for His disciples:
They are not of the world, even as I am not of the world. Sanctify them in the truth; Your word is truth. (John 17:16-17 NASB)

SANCTIFY:

basically 'set apart', like being set apart from everything else and dedicated to God only. Grace at salvation "sets the believer apart" as separate and holy unto God.

THOUGHTS:

So, Jesus is showing us that having God's Word, the Truth, in our hearts will set us apart from the world and make us holy.

Thank You Lord Jesus for praying for Your disciples as we live in this world and for reminding us over and over about the importance of God's Word for our sanctification.

O Father, You have given us the Word to be fully obeyed. Oh, that our ways were consistent in obeying! Then we would not be ashamed when we read Your Bible. According to Your Word So Be It.

This God—his way is perfect; the word of the Lord proves true; he is a shield for all those who take refuge in him. (Psalms 18:28,30 ESV)

GOD:

1. Way is perfect
2. His word is True
3. Shields all those who take refuge in Him

Dear God, our Lord and Father, You are our Light in this dark world. You lead us by a perfect way through Your Word that always is True. Fill our hearts with understanding and faith, so we will be obedient children, who run to You whenever we need help. Asking in Jesus Christ name may it be so.

Jesus said, "Blessed rather are those who hear the word of God and keep it!" (Luke 11:28 ESV)

O Father in this verse You have made it clear that we are to obey Your Word and not just listen and say that Oh that sounds good. Put false ways far from us and graciously teach us Your law! Cause us to be obedient in the narrow way of your commandments as You enlarge our hearts and bless us! In Jesus Christ name So Be It.

LINDA MCGREGOR CLARK

But don't just listen to God's word. You must do what it says. Otherwise, you are only fooling yourselves. (James 1:22-23 NLT)

GOD'S CHILDREN:

1. Listen and obey God's word
2. Do not fool ourselves

Heavenly Father give us understanding so we will obey Your instructions and put them into practice with all our hearts. Give us eagerness to obey Your laws! Turn our eyes from worthless things and give us life through Your word. Help us to be eager to keep Your commandments and to remember that the earth is full of Your love for Your children! In Jesus Christ name may it be so.

Hold firmly to the word of life. (Philippians 2:14-16 NLT)

GOD'S CHILDREN:

Hold firmly to God's word of life

O Lord, Your hands have made and fashioned us; give us understanding that we may learn Your commandments and hold firmly to Your word of life. Teach us good judgment and give us knowledge, then we will fear You and praise You rightly. Forgive us for being complaining children, who argue about things in our lives and many times want our own way. According to Your word So Be It.

My son, if you will receive my words And treasure my commandments within you, Make your ear attentive to wisdom, Incline your heart to understanding; Then you will discern the fear of the LORD And discover the knowledge of God. For the LORD gives wisdom; From His mouth come knowledge and understanding. (Proverbs 2:1-2, 5-6 NASB)

FEAR: worshiping God as truly awesome, profound deep reverence of God

GOD'S WORD:

1. Receive it and treasure it
2. Listen to it carefully
3. Concentrate on understanding
4. Teaches reverence toward God
5. Helps growth in knowledge of God through His wisdom
6. Helps us gain knowledge and understanding

Holy holy holy God, our Father, give us hearts that take in Your Word and treasure it. Give us understanding hearts that are in awe of You and are growing in knowledge of You through Your Word. Forgive us for being slack in reading the Bible. In Jesus Christ name So Be It.

So, faith comes from hearing, that is, hearing the Good News about Christ. (Romans 10:17 NLT)

GOOD NEWS is the Gospel and both terms mean the whole story about Jesus: that He is God, born as a man, lived a sinless life, taught God's truth, was crucified, dead and buried, then resurrected and sits at God's right hand and will return some day!

THOUGHTS:

Without God's Word, we would not know God, His plan, or our future! We would be in a terrible predicament! So, for the next three days, we will do a summary of what we have seen in our look at God's Word.

Dear Father, open our minds to understand the importance of the Bible and to treasure it as our life's guide. May our hearts be sound in Your statues so we will not be ashamed. In Jesus Christ name So Be It.

GOD'S WORD:

1. Living and active (Heb. 4:12 ESV)
2. Judges the thoughts and intentions of our hearts
3. Goes forth from God's mouth (Isa. 55:11 ESV)
4. Accomplishes exactly what God wants
5. Is God breathed (2Tim. 3:16-17 ESV)
6. Useful to:

    a. Teach true doctrine
    b. Correct wrongs
    c. Teach us to do right and be pleasing to God

7. God uses it to prepare and equip His children to do good works He has for us to do
8. Is settled forever in heaven (Ps. 119:89 ESV)
9. Is not a human message, but truly the Word of God
10. Is able to save souls
11. Holy men of God, led by the Holy Spirit, spoke God's word that we have today (2Peter 1:19-21 ESV)
12. Not one word of Scripture came from the will of man or from his own interpretation
13. All scriptures written were to teach us to endure and to have hope through Jesus
14. Is perfect and refreshes the soul (Rom. 15:4 ESV)
15. Trustworthy, right, reliable, precious, sweet, warns and obedience brings reward (Ps 19:7-11 ESV)

    (All the scripture references are from the ESV.)

O Father, what a wonderfully precious beginning descriptive list about Your Word! Open our eyes to see Your scriptures better and to understand them, so we will desire to be obedient children. Asking in Jesus Christ name So Be It.

LINDA MCGREGOR CLARK

GOD'S WORD:

"The Bible is not a 66-book position paper. It is not a divine thesis that lays out which of our human behaviors God "opposes" or "supports". The Bible is the authoritative word of a holy, just, and righteous God that mandates what sin is-period-regardless of our opinion." *Darrell B Harrison*

1. Is life to those who find it (Ps. 4:20-23 ESV)
2. Is the power of God to save all who believe (Rom. 1:16 ESV)
3. Never add to God's Word
4. Never take away from God's Word
5. Keep the commandments
6. Jesus did not abolish the Law, but fulfilled it
7. Will last without any changes till Heaven and earth pass away
8. Dangerous to disobey and to teach others to disobey (Matt. 5:17-19 ESV)
9. Rewards for obedience and for teaching others to obey
10. Is forever fixed in heaven (will not change)
11. Gives us life
12. Is God's perfect way (Ps. 18:30 ESV)
13. Proves to be True
14. Produces fruit
15. Sets God's children apart from the world (John 17:17 ESV)
    (All the scripture references are from the ESV)

Righteous are You, O LORD, and right are Your rules. Your testimonies are righteous forever and Your law is true. The sum of Your word is truth and every one of Your righteous rules endures forever. Thank You Father for giving us Your clear word, give us understanding as You teach us Your statues and set us apart by the fruit of our lives from those who don't know Your Word. According to Your Word So Be It.

"When reading God's Word we should keep in mind that we are reading the very words that came from God to enable us to know Him and to know His plan for our world. Also, think about who this God is, the One who created everything everywhere and even has names for all the millions of stars! On my phone, I have some pictures of birds taken by Bird Watchers and when I look at these pictures, I cannot imagine that God designed the colors and the feathers in the designs on each Wood Duck or Painted Bunting. If our God takes such precise effort with nature, then He will take extra special effort to make sure we get His exact words in His Bible, since He is telling us all about Himself and His Son and His plan for us.

GOD'S WORD:

1. Is light in darkness
2. Is perfect and proves to be true (Ps. 18:28,30 ESV)
3. Must listen and obey it (Jas.1:22 ESV)
   (All the scripture references are from the ESV)

THOUGHTS:

"There are moments when I'm so amazed by the holiness of God that I wonder why He permits these sinful hands of mine ever to touch the pages of His holy Word." *Darrell B. Harrison* I pray that we will develop this kind of attitude toward God's Word.

O Father please help us to love Your Word like we see in these quotes from Darrell Harrison. As we have gone through just a few scriptures, we've seen the importance of each verse as You open our eyes to see wonderful things in Your Law. Help us to always be governed by Your holy Word and May we receive the salvation which You have promised to those who believe in Jesus Christ the Savior, So Be It.

LINDA MCGREGOR CLARK

WHO IS A
CHRISTIAN?

After reading all about the importance of God's Bible and how it tells us how to live in a God pleasing way, now we will look at specific instructions for us to help us grow in our obedience. We will begin with Micah 6:8...

He has told you, O man, what is good; And what does the LORD require of you But to do justice, to love kindness, And to walk humbly with your God?
(Micah 6:8 NASB)

LORD REQUIRES OF US:

* To do justice (be impartial, righteous)Righteous means being right with God
* To love kindness (compassion, mercy)
* To live humbly with our God (not arrogant)

Merciful Lord, Fountain of All Righteousness help Your children to recognize when we are not living lives of righteousness and kindness and humility. Open our eyes to see our sin and to repent. Fill us with the fruit from the Holy Spirit of love, joy, peace, patience, kindness, goodness, faithfulness, gentleness and self-control. Asking through Jesus Christ Your Son, So Be It.

We are lying if we say we have fellowship with God but go on living in spiritual darkness But if we are living in the light, as God is in the light, then we have fellowship with each other, and the blood of Jesus, his Son, cleanses us from all sin. (1 John 1:5-7 NLT)

GOD's CHILDREN:

* Have fellowship with God
* Practice the truth
* Live in the light
* Fellowship with other children of God
* Blood of Jesus cleanses us from all our sins

LOST:

1. Have no fellowship with God
2. Live in spiritual darkness
3. Are not cleansed by Jesus's blood

Most Merciful Good and Gracious God, please give us hearts that believe and practice the Truth through our faith in Your Son Jesus Christ our Lord. Keep us from wandering from Your truth and open our eyes to understand it. Put the lies of the world away from us and teach us Your laws so we can live in the truth. Asking in Jesus Christ name, may it be so.

LINDA MCGREGOR CLARK

If we confess our sins to God, he is faithful and just to forgive us our sins and to cleanse us from all wickedness. If we claim we have not sinned, we are calling God a liar and showing that his word has no place in our hearts. (1 John 1:9-10 NLT)

GOD'S CHILDREN:

1. Know we sin
2. Live in the Truth
3. Confess our sins to God
4. Are forgiven
5. God's Word is in our hearts

LOST:

1. Are sinners
2. Claim they do not sin
3. Do not have God's Word in their hearts

Heavenly Father You are full of Mercy and as we look at the things You require of us, we ask that You give us eyes to see our sins and then hearts to repent, so we can fellowship with You in Your Word and be obedient to Your commandments, while living in the Truth. According to Your Word So Be It.

If anyone does sin, we have an advocate who pleads our case before the Father. He is Jesus Christ, the one who is truly righteous. He himself is the sacrifice that atones for our sins— and not only our sins but the sins of all the world. (1 John 2:1-2 NLT)

JESUS IS:

- The Advocate for God's children, who stands in our place before the Father
- Truly Righteous
- The Sacrifice that pays for our sins and for the sins of the whole world

Good and Gracious God forgive all our many sins and Holy Spirit govern our lives, so we will be obedient to The Father God's commandments and live our lives in humble submission to God. In Jesus Christ name Amen

LINDA MCGREGOR CLARK

Those who say they live in God should live their lives as Jesus did. (1 John 2:3-6 NLT)

GOD's CHILDREN:

* Obey God's commandments
* Live in the Truth
* Love God
* Live as Jesus did

O Lord, we have a long way to go to be the obedient children You require and You have commanded that Your precepts should be kept diligently, help us to be steadfast in obeying. Also remember You have promised that once You've begun a good work in us, You will complete it. Help us to live as Jesus did. According to Your Word So Be It.

And this is God's commandment: We must believe in the name of his Son, Jesus Christ, and love one another, just as he commanded us. (1 John 3:23 NLT)

GOD'S CHILDREN:

1. Believe in the name of Jesus Christ
2. Love each other
3. Are obedient to God's commands

Dear Father, we believe in Jesus Christ Your Son and we do love other believers, but sometimes we get frustrated or impatient with our brothers and sisters. Forgiveness is something that Jesus said we are to do 70X70 times. Forgive us for not always being forgiving.

O Holy Spirit give us soft, humble hearts full of mercy so that we will be obedient, loving, forgiving children, who are in fellowship with our Father, through Jesus's name So Be It.

LINDA MCGREGOR CLARK

Blessed be the God and Father of our Lord Jesus Christ. Because of his great mercy he has given us new birth into a living hope through the resurrection of Jesus Christ from the dead. (1 Peter 1:1-5 CSB)

CHOSEN:

1. God is our Father
2. Has mercy on us
3. Given new birth
4. Given hope through Jesus' resurrection from the dead

WOW Precious Heavenly Father, You have done totally awesome underserved things for Your children! Give us understanding and wisdom to use these gifts for Your Glory, as we get to know Your laws and statues and commandments. Open our eyes to see our sins and to turn to You in repentance and to be obedient. In Jesus Precious Name So Be It.

But as the one who called you is holy, you also are to be holy in all your conduct; for it is written, Be holy, because I am holy. (1 Peter 1:14-16 CSB)

HOLY GOD:

Exalted and worthy of complete devotion as One perfect in goodness and righteousness

HOLY CHILD:

1. Set apart from all else and devoted entirely to God
2. Obedient
3. Do not live to satisfy our own desires, like we did before
4. Holy in all our conduct

Dear Heavenly Father this requirement that we be Holy like You is impossible unless You change our hearts since our hearts are so selfish. Please do a deep work in us and cause us to love the things You love and to Hate what You Hate. Asking because of Jesus Amen

LINDA MCGREGOR CLARK

As I have talked to different people lately, I have come to realize that most people have no idea what sin is and how serious it is in God's eyes. So, I decided we all need a refresher course on sin to understand why God hates it and for us to know why repentance is so important in our lives.

It is sin to know what you ought to do and then not do it. (James 4:17 NLT)

Everyone who makes a practice of sinning also practices lawlessness, sin is lawlessness. (1 John 3:4 ESV)

THOUGHTS:

These verses show us how serious sin is with a Holy, Just God, Who hates sin and requires blood to be shed to pay the price for it. Yet we do not call sin "sin", but we use words like mistake, slip up, error, shortcomings, failure and others. But God has clearly shown us that sin is lawlessness. Now that's serious and exactly why Jesus's sacrifice was so important. Because when we repent and are washed in His blood, our sins are forgiven and, also, Jesus is the only way to God's forgiveness there is no other.

Holy, Holy, Holy God Who has given us our primary purpose for living, which is to glorify You and enjoy You forever. Good and upright are You Lord; therefore, instruct us sinners in the narrow way and teach us humility to follow Your way. So, we will see our sins, repent and be washed in Jesus's blood. We ask in the name of Your Son Christ Jesus So Be It.

I said, "I will confess my transgressions to the LORD "; And You forgave the guilt of my sin. (Psalms 32: 5 NASB)

SIN:

1. *Transgression:* an act that goes against God's law, rule or code of conduct
2. *Iniquity:* immoral behavior or grossly unfair behavior, wickedness

Help, O God of our salvation and for the glory of Your name, make us aware of our sins, deliver us from them and forgive our sins for Your name's sake. Bless us and wash us thoroughly from our sin in Jesus's blood. So Be It.

Your iniquities have made a separation between you and your God, and your sins have hidden His face from you so that He does not hear. (Isaiah 59:1-2 NASB)

O God, Creator of all things, thank You for hearing our prayers of repentance and for not hiding Your face from us as the Holy Spirit helps us understand these verses clearly, and helps us to be quick to recognize our sins and then to repent, so we won't be separated from You because of our sins. Through Jesus Christ, our only Savior Amen

He has not dealt with us according to our sins, nor rewarded us according to our iniquities. For as high as the heavens are above the earth, so great is His lovingkindness toward those who fear Him. As far as the east is from the west, so far has He removed our transgressions from us. (Psalms 103:10-12 NASB)

GOD:

1. Does not deal with us according to our sins
2. Does not reward us according to our iniquities
3. Removes our transgressions from us

SIN: Breaking God's laws
INIQUITY: wicked acts
TRANSGRESSION: Crime, lawbreaking, violations

Just and Righteous Judge of all the world thank You for not dealing with us according to our many sins because Jesus paid the price for our sins through His life, death and resurrection. Thank You for Your great lovingkindness toward those who are in awe of You and for removing our sins away from us. Keep us ever aware of our sins and because of our fear of You make us repent by means of the blood of Christ Jesus Your Son, So Be It.

For all have sinned and fall short of the glory of God.
(Romans 3:23 ESV)

Without the shedding of blood there is no forgiveness of sins.
(Hebrews 9:22 ESV)

GOD:

1. Glorious
2. Loves His chosen people
3. Hates sin
4. Died for us

GOD'S CHILDREN:

1. All have sinned
2. Loved by God
3. Christ died for us

In these two verses we see that breaking God's laws and participating in wicked acts bring out God's Wrath that requires Propitiation by Jesus's blood. This means that Jesus's sacrifice on the Cross *satisfied* God's Wrath against our sins by His suffering and shedding His blood, which we must receive by faith.

O Father, these are such deep warnings and yet wonderful facts about what You've done to rescue us from Your wrath through propitiation by Jesus's blood. Give us understanding to recognize our sins and to repent then give us the faith to be obedient children, according to Your Commandments So Be It.

LINDA MCGREGOR CLARK

God's Commandments are found in Exodus 20. We will go through these and apply them to our lives for the next 10 devotions in order to better recognize our sins, then be able to repent and turn away from them.

(1)"You shall have no other gods before me. (Exodus 20:2-3 ESV)

THOUGHTS:

God begins the 10 Commandments by reminding us Who He is and what He has done for us. He is The LORD our God, our Redeemer, Who rescued us from being slaves to sin. Therefore, we must keep His all commandments.

The first commandment requires us to know and recognize God as the only true God and worship and to glorify Him properly
Westminster Shorter Catechism Modern English

O God our Lord Who sees everything and Who hates it if we love anyone or anything more then You show us where we've committed this sin of loving other things or people more than You, give us repentant hearts and help us be obedient children. In Jesus Christ name So Be It.

(2)"**Y**ou shall not make for yourself a carved image, or any likeness of anything that is in heaven above, or that is in the earth beneath, or that is in the water under the earth. (Exodus 20:4-5 ESV)

THOUGHTS:

Here God forbids us to worship God with images or statues or in any other way except what is explained and shown in His Word. So, we see this is serious and that God wants us to worship exactly as He expects and it is sin when we worship in the wrong way.

Heavenly Father, we will praise You and worship You with upright hearts, when we learn Your righteous rules. Yet we are a very visual people and desire to be able to see or touch or hold the things we love. Forgive us Father and teach us the right way to worship, the God pleasing way. According to Your Word So Be It.

LINDA MCGREGOR CLARK

(3)"You shall not take the name of the Lord your God in vain, for the Lord will not hold him guiltless who takes his name in vain. (Exodus 20:7 ESV)

THOUGHTS:

This commandment requires the holy and reverent use of God's names, His titles, His Word and His works, anything God uses to make Himself known and Oh My how we break this law every day!

O God, we are people with unclean mouths and live among people with unclean mouths and we have sinned with our words! Please forgive us and cleanse our hearts,and open our ears to hear, so our tongues will obey this commandment. In Jesus Christ name Amen

(4)"**R**emember the Sabbath day, to keep it holy.
(Exodus 20:8 ESV)

THOUGHTS:

This commandment requires us to set apart this day to worship God, and to rest from work. For Christians this is the first day of the week.

O Father thank You for this special day that we can rest and go to church to worship and grow in our knowledge of You. Help us to remember this is not only a commandment, but a gift too. Forgive us when we treat Your Day like any other day and don't find a time to focus on and worship You. In Jesus Christ name Amen

---

(5)"**H**onor your father and your mother. (Exodus 20:12 ESV)

THOUGHTS:

The 5th Commandment requires us to be respectful toward our parents and toward all with whom we come in contact. We are not to be disrespectful to others and are to glorify God by our behavior.

Holy Spirit fill our hearts with Your love, our lips with gentle, helpful words and our hands with respectful, kind, unselfish deeds. So that others will know that we are God's children. Because of Jesus Christ, our Lord So Be It.

LINDA MCGREGOR CLARK

(6)"You shall not murder. (Exodus 20:13 ESV)

Jesus teaching His disciples about the importance of keeping the commandments not just outwardly but in our hearts and minds:

You have heard that our ancestors were told, 'You must not murder. If you commit murder, you are subject to judgment.' But I say, if you are even angry with someone, you are subject to judgment! (Matthew 5:21-22 NLT)

O Father God, we read this commandment and think "this is one I can easily obey." But Jesus points out that it goes deeper than our actions and we sin through hate in our hearts and by the words we speak, just as if we had killed that person. Now that's a lot harder to obey because we are easily angered. Help us to see our selfishness which feeds this anger and then fill our hearts with repentance and with Your love through Your Son Jesus Christ So Be It.

(7) **Y**ou shall not commit adultery. (Exodus 20:14 NASB)

Jesus teaching:

You have heard that it was said, 'YOU SHALL NOT COMMIT ADULTERY '; but I say to you that everyone who looks at a woman with lust for her has already committed adultery with her in his heart. (Matthew 5:27-28 NASB)

THOUGHTS:

This commandment requires the preservation of our own and our neighbor's purity, in heart, speech, and behavior. It forbids all unchaste thoughts, words and actions.(Westminster Shorter Catechism)

Adultery is voluntary unfaithfulness between a married person and someone other than that person's spouse. God requires us to always be faithful to our commitments. Anything else is a sin and this commandment is for both males and females.

O Father, Jesus taught clearly that to obey Your commandments we must begin with examining our hearts, because all our sinful desires and actions begin there. Open our eyes to see our sin and help us to repent. We are surrounded by people who call evil good and good evil. Protect us by the pure truth of Your Word. In Christ Jesus name, So Be It.

LINDA MCGREGOR CLARK

(8) "You shall not steal."(Exodus 20:15 NASB)

THOUGHTS:

This commandment requires us to lawfully attain and expand our own wealth and estate for ourselves or for others.Yet we live among people who say, "Follow your heart." This world's way of living is exactly the opposite of what God tells us in the Bible. So, we must be careful to guard against the false ideas of the world about what is ours or what we deserve or what others do not deserve.

Dear Holy Spirit, our Comforter and Teacher, help us to recognize when we're breaking God's laws. Then give us repentant hearts and fill us with the desire to be obedient children of God. According to Your Word So Be It.

(9)"You shall not bear false witness against your neighbor."
(Exodus 20:16 NASB).

THOUGHTS:

The 9th commandment requires us to tell the truth and to keep it going, so that nothing gets in the way of truth or injures another's reputation.

Here is another instance of God's rules being the opposite from the world. We see every day on TV, in All Social media, that this world is full of lies used to destroy others. We must be incredibly careful with our words!

O Father make us truly aware of our sinfulness, fill us with hate of our sins and sadness over them and give us deeply repentant hearts that strive to be obedient to Your laws. Keep us from following the world's way, which is the broad way that leads to destruction and keep us on the narrow path that leads to life. Because of Jesus Amen

LINDA MCGREGOR CLARK

(10) "You shall not covet. (Exodus 20:17 NASB)

THOUGHTS:

The 10th Commandment is warning us against wanting anything that belongs to someone else and wishing they did not have it. Because everything we have comes from God, we should be fully satisfied with His good gifts that He has given to us.

Dear Lord, every catalog, every commercial is created to make us dissatisfied with our lives and we fall in the trap over and over! Help us to be wise and to focus on the wonderful gifts You've already given to us. Forgive us for coveting what our eyes see and make us completely satisfied in our lives. In the name of Jesus Christ Amen

We've looked at God's 10 Commandments:

1. *You shall have no other gods before Me.*
2. *You shall not make for yourself any idols*
3. *You shall not misuse the name of the LORD your God; the LORD will hold you guilty.*
4. *Remember the Sabbath Day by keeping it holy.*
5. *Honor your Father and your Mother.*
6. *You shall not murder.*
7. *You shall not commit adultery.*
8. *You shall not steal.*
9. *You shall not give false testimony.*
10. *You shall not covet.*

To escape from God's wrath over our sins, we must turn to Jesus in faith for salvation, be truly sorry for our sins and really try to be obedient by using all the means God has given us to grow in faith, like the Bible, prayer and fellowship with other Christians daily and attend church.

O Holy Spirit our Counselor and Teacher as we've gone through God's commandments, please give us eyes to see our sin and hearts that are very sad over our thoughts and desires and words. Help us to turn away from our sins and to turn toward pleasing our Father. Praying according to God's Grace and Mercy, So Be It.

LINDA MCGREGOR CLARK

In the sermon on the mount, Jesus taught His disciples about the importance of God's commandments:

Do not think that I have come to abolish the Law or the Prophets; I have not come to abolish them but to fulfill them. For truly, I say to you, until heaven and earth pass away, not an iota, not a dot, will pass from the Law until all is accomplished. (Matthew 5:17-18 ESV)

THOUGHTS:

Jesus was truly clear that we are to continue to make every effort to obey God's commandments. Also, He made sure we understand that the commandments go deeper to include our thoughts and feelings, not just what we do.

Dear Jesus, Son of God, God Incarnate, we are slowly learning what is required of God's children and realizing how far off the mark we are! Thank You for making forgiveness possible through our faith in You and through God's mercy and grace. Thank You for suffering alone and shedding Your blood to satisfy God's Wrath against our sins, of which we are completely undeserving! In Your name, we pray, Amen

Teacher, which is the most important commandment in the law of God? Jesus replied, You must love the LORD your God with all your heart, all your soul, and all your mind. This is the first and greatest commandment. A second is equally important: 'Love your neighbor as yourself. The entire law and all the demands of the prophets are based on these two commandments. (Matthew 22:36-40 NLT)

THOUGHTS:

At first when we read this it seems to be another commandment. But Jesus is summarizing the law by saying the entire law is based on Loving God totally and loving others as we love ourselves.

1. The first four commandments are more specific about our relationship to God, so loving Him with all our heart, soul and mind would result in our deep desire to obey them.
2. The next six commandments concern our relationships with others, which would make each of these important to us as we love others like we love ourselves.
3. But all God's law is based (founded; made important to us) on love of God and love of others.

O Holy Spirit, we are so far from loving the way Jesus has described we should love God and love our neighbors. We need real repentance and much forgiveness then fill our hearts with God's true love. So, we will love God completely and love others as God loves us. In Jesus Christ name Amen

LINDA MCGREGOR CLARK

Today I want to share a little of my personal journey with you as I have been studying and praying to be able to share these devotions with you. I pray you have been touched like me.

A new commandment I give to you, that you love one another, even as I have loved you, that you also love one another. By this all men will know that you are My disciples, if you have love for one another.(John 13:34-35 NASB)

So, you must live as God's obedient children. Do not slip back into your old ways of living to satisfy your own desires...But now you must be holy in everything you do, just as God who chose you is holy. For the Scriptures say, "YOU MUST BE HOLY BECAUSE I AM HOLY." (1 Peter 1:14-16 NLT)

As I have studied the 10 Commandments more diligently these last two weeks along with other scriptures, I have begun to see my own many sins.Then as I read what Jesus said about His disciples needing to live lives of sacrificial love like He did, I see my selfishness and realize I need much repentance! Also, the verses on being holy bring conviction to me and caused me deep sadness. But then excitement comes as I am reminded of God's Grace that is available to me because of the Blood of Jesus that was shed for the sins of the world! I have been saved from God's Wrath and from the punishment for my sins by faith in Christ Jesus, Who is the propitiation for my sins. Hallelujah!!

PROPITIATION: Jesus's sacrifice was the needed payment to _satisfy_ God's Wrath and to cover the cost of my sins, for without the shedding of blood, there is no forgiveness of sins.

"Oh Father, thank You, thank You, thank You for loving me and sending Your Son to be the propitiation for my sins! I am so sorry that I have not loved You with all my heart and mind and soul and strength or my neighbor as myself. Nor have I loved the sacrificial way that Jesus loved, nor am I even close to being holy! Oh, but I do want to grow in love and holiness, so Holy Spirit fill me with holiness and deep love for God and for others. According to Your Word So Be It."

This is a personal prayer, and you can use it for yourself or you can make your own prayer as the Holy Spirit leads you, since God works differently with each of His children.

My prayer for you is the you will understand the Words you're reading, will grow in your knowledge of God our Father and Christ Jesus our Lord, that your heart will be challenged to change, repentance will come and you will be blessed by God! May it be so!

LINDA MCGREGOR CLARK

WHO IS JESUS?

Jesus is the image of the invisible God...For by him all things were created, in heaven and on earth, visible and invisible, whether thrones or dominions or rulers or authorities—all things were created through Jesus and for him. And he is before all things, and in him all things hold together. And he is the head of the body, the church. Jesus is the beginning, the firstborn from the dead, that in everything he might be preeminent. For in Jesus all the fullness of God was pleased to dwell. (Colossians 1:15-19 ESV)

JESUS:

1. the image of the invisible God
2. by Him ALL things were created in heaven and on earth
3. all things were created through Him and for Him and without Him nothing was made
4. He is before all things
5. He holds all things together
6. He is the Head of the church
7. He is the 1st person to be raised from the dead
8. He is preeminent (Supreme, Sovereign over ALL)
9. all the fullness of God lives in Him.

WHY IS THIS IMPORTANT:

What we know and understand about Jesus is eternally important because belief in Him is the only way to eternal life in heaven.

O Lord Jesus, what a wonderful, wonderful, wonderful description of who You are, God Almighty!!

O Holy Spirit get these truths deeply into our hearts and protect us from the lies of false teachers.

Thank You Father God for giving us the Word, the Truth, the Perfect revelation of who Jesus is. So that as we know Jesus better, we will grow to know You better. In the name of God, the Son, Jesus Christ So Be It

LINDA MCGREGOR CLARK

For in Christ lives all the fullness of God in a human body. So, you also are complete through your union with Christ, who is the head over every ruler and authority. (Colossians 2:8-10 NLT)

JESUS:

1. is fully a man and fully God
2. makes us complete by living in us
3. is Head over every ruler and every authority

WHY IS THIS IMPORTANT:

Jesus told us that He is the only way to God.

Dearest Lord Jesus, it is a wonderful blessing to look and learn and be reminded of Who You are! Now today the false teachers are saying that You are not God but only a man. Help us see these Truths that are taught to us by the Bible, which say You are fully man and fully God and You live in us by the Holy Spirit! Give us understanding and faith! In Your most Holy, Powerful, Gracious and Merciful Name So Be It

In these last days God has spoken to us by his Son, whom he appointed the heir of all things, through whom also he created the world. He is the radiance of the glory of God and the exact imprint of God's nature, and he upholds the universe by the word of his power. After making purification for sins (on the cross), he sat down at the right hand of the Majesty on high. (Hebrews 1:1-3 ESV)

WHO IS JESUS:

1. God speaks through Him to us
2. He is Heir of all things
3. the universe was created by Him
4. radiates God's glory
5. is the exact representation of God
6. sustains the universe by His mighty power
7. made us pure by His sacrifice
8. Now He's sitting at God's right hand.

WHY IS THIS IMPORTANT:

Jesus said, "this is the work of God—that you believe in the one He has sent." (John 6:29 CSB)

Dearest Lord Jesus, thank You that we can know You better through the true words of the Bible. What wonderful truths we've been reading so far!! Give us deep faith and trust as we learn that You are God the Son, also, teach us that as we get to know You better, we will know God better. Praying in the Mighty name Amen

LINDA MCGREGOR CLARK

To the Son he says, "Your throne, O God, endures forever and ever. You rule with a scepter of justice...He also says to the Son, "In the beginning, Lord, you laid the foundation of the earth and made the heavens with your hands. They will perish, but you remain forever. (Hebrews 1:8, 10-12 NLT)

WHO IS JESUS:

1. is God the Son
2. His throne endures forever
3. He rules in justice
4. He is Lord
5. laid the foundation of the earth
6. made the heavens with His hands
7. is always the same
8. lives forever

WHY IS THIS IMPORTANT:

Now this is God's command that we believe in the name of His Son, Jesus Christ, and love one another, but both things are impossible unless we know the Truth about Jesus.

O Lord Jesus, it is so amazing that You, the God Who created and rules over all things, would even take notice of us! Yet You left the glory of heaven, took the body of a man, suffered all the humiliation, including the terrible pain and sacrifice of death on the cross, so we sinners and enemies can live in heaven with You! O Holy Spirit teach us the whole truth and give us understanding, so we will grow in faith and help us recognize any false beliefs about Jesus, so we will worship Him fully. In the name of God the Son Amen

In the beginning was the Word, and the Word was with God, and the Word was God. He was with God in the beginning. All things were created through him, and apart from him not one thing was created that has been created. In him was life, and that life was the light of men. That light shines in the darkness, and yet the darkness cannot overcome it. (John 1:1-5 CSB)

WHO IS JESUS:

1. is the Word of God
2. is from the beginning (Eternal)
3. is God
4. all things were created through Him
5. apart from Him not one thing was created that has been created
6. in Him is Life
7. is the Light
8. He shines in the darkness of this world
9. the darkness (evil) cannot overcome Him.

WHY IS THIS IMPORTANT:

For there is one God, and there is one mediator between God and men, the man Christ Jesus, who gave Himself as a ransom for all... (1Tim. 2:5 NKJV)

O Father God, this information is so wonderful! Thank You for sending Jesus to save us from Your wrath over our many sins, even when we were Your enemies!

O Lord Jesus, getting to know You better and to know the Truth about You is fantastic! Thank You for being the exact representation of God, so we can know God better and worship Him in a God pleasing way.

LINDA MCGREGOR CLARK

O Holy Spirit give us minds to understand the Truth and hearts to believe and obey.

We pray all this in the name of the Light of the world, Jesus Christ So Be It.

The true light, which gives light to everyone, He was in the world, and the world was made through him, to all who did receive him, who believed in his name, he gave the right to become children of God. (John 1:9-12 ESV)

WHO IS JESUS:

1. is the True Light
2. gives light to everyone
3. was in the world, which was made through Him
4. most people do not believe in Jesus
5. He came to the Jews and they did not receive Him
6. all who believe in His name become the children of God.

WHY IS THIS IMPORTANT:

Everyone who believes in Jesus receives forgiveness of sins.

O Father God, more wonderful Truth for us to believe and by which to live! Help us to both, believe that Jesus is God and obey His teaching!

O Lord Jesus, fill us with Your Light, so we will shine in this unbelieving world, then many more people will become children of God.

Through the name of the True Light of the world, Jesus Christ So Be It.

LINDA MCGREGOR CLARK

The Word became flesh and dwelt among us, and we have seen his glory, glory of the only Son from the Father, full of grace and truth. (John 1:14 ESV)

WHO IS JESUS:

1. is the Word in the flesh
2. lived on earth
3. people saw His glory(greatness)
4. Son of God the Father
5. full of grace (forgiveness and power) and Truth.

WHY IS THIS IMPORTANT:

There is salvation in no one else; for there is no other name under heaven that has been given among men, by which we must be saved. (Acts 4:12 NASB)

O Holy Spirit, our Teacher, fill our hearts with understanding of the Truth that Jesus is God and yet He was fully man. Help us to grow in faith, trust, repentance and love. These many truths about Jesus are so important that we need Your guidance to correct any false ideas we have about Jesus, then increase our knowledge of Him because there are so many lies in our world about Jesus. Through Jesus Christ name Amen

God's unfailing love and faithfulness came through Jesus Christ. No one has ever seen God. But the one and only Son, who is himself God, is near to the Father's heart. He has revealed God to us. (John 1:16-18 NLT)

WHO IS JESUS:

1. God's unfailing love and faithfulness come to us through Jesus
2. only Jesus has ever seen God
3. is the One and Only Son
4. is God Himself
5. is near to God the Father's heart
6. reveals God to us.

WHY IS THIS IMPORTANT:

Because if we believe that Jesus is God the Son, then we will be saved.

O Jesus, thank You so much for revealing our Heavenly Father to us as we get to know You better through these verses! Thank You for showing us God's unfailing love and unfailing faithfulness and for giving us grace and more grace! We're so undeserving of anything from You, but You chose us before we were born!! Keep us near and fill us with faith! In Your Precious Name So Be It

LINDA MCGREGOR CLARK

The next day John saw Jesus coming toward him and said, "Look! The Lamb of God who takes away the sin of the world. (John 1:29,32-34 NLT)

WHO IS JESUS:

1. is the Lamb of God Who takes away the sins of the world
2. He baptizes with the Holy Spirit
3. is God the Son.

WHY IS THIS IMPORTANT:

If we believe that Jesus is God'd Lamb, then we will be saved.

Dearest Lamb of God, thank You for coming to earth and living here, so You could make it possible for sinners like us to have our sins removed!! Thank You for baptizing us, when we believe, with the Holy Spirit to teach us and lead us on the narrow path!

Thank You Holy Spirit for being our comforter, teacher and guide, as we live on earth. Give us ears to hear, hearts to understand and wills to obey, so we will grow to be more and more like Jesus.

We praise You Father God!!! So Be It.

These are Jesus's words about Himself and His mission on earth:

The Son of Man has come down from heaven. And as Moses lifted up the bronze snake on a pole in the wilderness (for the people to look at and be healed), so the Son of Man must be lifted up, so that everyone who believes in him will have eternal life. (John 3:13-15 NLT)

WHO IS JESUS:

1. is the Son of man (fully man and fully God)
2. came down from Heaven to earth
3. was lifted up on the cross, so that everyone who believes in Him will have eternal life in Heaven.

WHY IS THIS IMPORTANT:

Jesus made it clear that He would be lifted up on the Cross so we who believe can have eternal life.

O Lord Jesus, thank You so much for leaving Your perfect, holy heaven to come to this dark, evil earth, then to be humiliated, suffer and die, all because we are lost sinners, who need saving from God's wrath! That's an enormous amount of love!! We will never know the depth of Your love. Help us to understand as much as possible.
O Holy Spirit, our minds are so full of wrong thinking, please give us understanding, faith and the desire to follow and trust Jesus with our lives. In Jesus Christ name Amen

LINDA MCGREGOR CLARK

*M*ore words spoken by Jesus explaining Who His is:

"For God so loved the world, that he gave his only Son, that whoever believes in him should not perish but have eternal life. For God did not send his Son into the world to condemn the world, but in order that the world might be saved through him. Whoever believes in him is not condemned, but whoever does not believe is condemned already, because he has not believed in the name of the only Son of God. (John 3:16-18 ESV)

WHO IS JESUS:

1. given by God the Father to the world, because of God's love
2. makes eternal life in heaven possible for us
3. must be believed in as God the Son
4. came not to condemn but to save
5. believers are not condemned
6. unbelievers are condemned
7. is the only Son of God.

SAVED:

1. Loved by God
2. Believe in God's only Son
3. Have eternal life
4. Saved through Jesus
5. Not condemned

WHY IS THIS IMPORTANT:

Without faith in Jesus, we would be condemned.

O Father, thank You for loving us sinners so much that You sent Jesus to rescue us from Your wrath over our many sins!

Thank You Jesus for paying for our condemnation, so we can have eternal life in heaven!

O Holy Spirit help us understand the Truth and to believe in the name of the Only Eternal Son of God, Jesus Christ, So Be It

LINDA MCGREGOR CLARK

For the Son is sent by God. He speaks God's words, for God gives him the Spirit without limit. The Father loves his Son and has put everything into his hands. And anyone who believes in God's Son has eternal life. Anyone who doesn't obey the Son will never experience eternal life but remains under God's wrath." (John 3:34-36 NLT)

WHO IS JESUS:

1. is the Son sent by God
2. speaks God's words
3. has the Holy Spirit without limit
4. is loved by God
5. has power over all things
6. all who believe in Him have eternal life
7. anyone who does not believe will not have eternal life but remains under God's wrath.

WHY IS THIS IMPORTANT:

God expects us to believe in His Son and when we do, we get eternal life. If a person does not believe and obey Jesus then he will be under God's wrath.

Dear loving, gracious God, help us to understand the Truth of the words explaining who Jesus is and what He's done for us. Give us faith to trust and obey His words that are Your words. Open our eyes to recognize whether we are on the narrow road or if we have gotten off it. And Father, please help all our family and friends to believe too! In Jesus Christ name Amen

Jesus returned to Jerusalem near the Sheep Gate was the pool of Bethesda. One of the men lying there had been sick for thirty-eight years...Jesus told him, "Stand up, pick up your mat, and walk!" Instantly, the man was healed! He rolled up his sleeping mat and began walking! But this miracle happened on the Sabbath, so the Jewish leaders objected. Then Jewish leaders began harassing Jesus for breaking the Sabbath rules. But Jesus replied, "My Father is always working, and so am I." So, the Jewish leaders tried all the harder to find a way to kill him. For he not only broke the Sabbath, he called God his Father, thereby making himself equal with God. (John 5:1-18 NLT)

WHO IS JESUS:

1. has the power to heal with a word
2. Jewish leaders hated Jesus so much that they did not care that a man was healed
3. Jewish leaders planned to kill Him
4. He called God His Father, making Himself equal with God
5. said He does the things that His Father does
6. everything He said made Himself equal with God and all who heard Him understood what He was saying.

WHY IS THIS IMPORTANT:

In this time which we live there is much wrong information and lies on who Jesus is, so it is very important that we know exactly what the Bible says and what Jesus said about Himself.

O Holy Spirit, You are our guide and teacher! Help us to fully understand Jesus's words, so we will be able to follow Him, to trust Him and to worship Him correctly. Protect us from the lies of those who hate Jesus.

O Father God, thank You for loving us and giving us new hearts to believe the Truth! Lead us, O Lord, in Your righteous Truth. Praying in Jesus Christ Name Amen

So, Jesus said to the religious leaders, "Truly, truly, I say to you, the Son can do nothing of his own accord, but only what he sees the Father doing. For whatever the Father does, that the Son does likewise. For as the Father raises the dead and gives them life, so also the Son gives life to whom he will. Whoever does not honor the Son does not honor the Father who sent him. Truly, truly, I say to you, whoever hears my word and believes God who sent me has eternal life. He does not come into judgment but has passed from death to life. (John 5:19-24 ESV)

WHO IS JESUS:

1. does exactly what His Father does
2. is loved by His Father
3. has the authority to do great works
4. gives life to anyone He chooses
5. has all authority to judge and should be honored
6. words are True, must be believed, then we receive eternal life and won't come under judgement, but will pass from death to life.

SAVED:

1. Have life from Jesus
2. Honor the Son
3. Honor the Father
4. Hears Jesus's words and believe God sent Him
5. Have eternal live
6. Do not come into judgment
7. Passed from death to life

WHY IS THIS IMPORTANT:

Because believing in Jesus is the only way to heaven.

O Father, the more we read about Jesus, the more wonderful it is to know that He, God the Son, made it possible for us not to be judged but to be in heaven with Him forever! Give us thankful, faithful hearts and keep us close during this time in which we live. In the name of the Judge and Savior Jesus Christ So Be It

Jesus speaking:

I can do nothing on my own. I judge as God tells me. Therefore, my judgment is just, because I carry out the will of God my Father, who sent me, not my own will. You search the Scriptures because you think they give you eternal life. But the Scriptures point to me. I have come to you in my Father's name, and you have rejected me. (John 5:30-43 NLT)

WHO IS JESUS:

1. did nothing on His own, but only His Father's will
2. judges as God judges
3. seeks not His own will, but the Father's will
4. sent by God the Father
5. Scriptures point to Jesus
6. He came in His Father's name
7. He was rejected by the religious leaders but gives eternal life to all who come to Him.

WHY IS THIS IMPORTANT:

Because there is only one God and only one go-between for us to approach God and that is Jesus.

O Father, help us remember the wonderful gift You gave to Your children, turn our eyes away from worthless things and turn our focus onto Jesus. Forgive us for not living lives that are pleasing to You. Holy Spirit open our minds and hearts to understand the words of Jesus so we can trust and obey Him! O Jesus, Thank You so much for coming to earth to die for us and save us from God's wrath! Praying according to God's Word, So Be It

Jesus said, "I am the bread of life. Whoever comes to me will never be hungry again. Whoever believes in me will never be thirsty. (John 6:35 NLT)

WHO IS JESUS:

1. is the Bread of life
2. will never reject believers
3. anyone who believes has eternal life
4. offered His flesh, so believers will live forever.

WHY IS THIS IMPORTANT:

Anyone who believes in the name of Jesus will be saved.

O Father, this verse explains that Jesus's work was to reveal to us that He is God the Son and that faith in Him is the way to eternal life. O Holy Spirit give us faith to understand who Jesus is and to believe, so we may have eternal life. In Jesus Christ name Amen

Jesus said, "If anyone is thirsty, let him come to Me and drink. He who believes in Me, as the Scripture said, 'From his innermost being will flow rivers of living water.'" By this Jesus spoke of the Holy Spirit, whom those who believed in Jesus were to receive; for the Holy Spirit was not yet given, because Jesus was not yet glorified. (John 7:37-39 NASB)

WHO IS JESUS:

1. gives believers the Holy Spirit
2. is now glorified
3. sent the Holy Spirit

WHO IS THE HOLY SPIRIT:

1. lives in believers
2. is our Comforter
3. teaches us all about Jesus
4. helps us remember scripture and all that we've been taught about Jesus
5. convicts us of sin
6. fills us with joy and hope
7. helps us grow in holiness.

WHY IS THIS IMPORTANT:

God has commanded that we believe in His Son Jesus Christ.

O Lord Jesus, thank You, thank You for the Holy Spirit, Who now lives in us to be our Comforter in times of sorrow and to teach us all we need to know about You to be saved from God's wrath over our sins. Thank You Holy Spirit for convicting us of our sins, then filling us with hope and joy and growing our faith through our daily repentance.
According to the Word of God So Be It!

LINDA MCGREGOR CLARK

Jesus spoke to the people once more and said, "I am the light of the world. Whoever follows me, shall not walk in darkness, but shall have the light of life." (John 8:12 ESV)

WHO IS JESUS:

1. is the Light of the world
2. Light leads believers to eternal life
3. Light of Good News (Gospel) is about Jesus being exactly God.

WHY IS THIS IMPORTANT:

Because Jesus is the only Light who will lead us out of the dark world.

O Father, thank You for opening our minds to the Light, so we can understand the Good News about Jesus! Help us to grow in our understanding and to really shine with the Light of Jesus, so unbelievers will want the Light too. In Jesus Christ name Amen

Anyone who belongs to God listens gladly to the words of God. But if you don't listen it's because you don't belong to God." (John 8:47 NLT)

So far, we have seen and read this Truth about Jesus:

1. He is the Eternal Creator of all things in heaven, on earth and under the earth
2. He is fully God and fully Man
3. He has the exact same character as God
4. He is Himself God
5. He reveals God to us
6. He is the Only Son of God, Not created, but Creator
7. referred to Himself as I AM, the Name that God said was His name
8. He made Himself equal with God
9. belief in Him is the only way to enter heaven for eternity

These are a few of the many true statements about Jesus in the Bible. The most important things for us to remember are He is the only way to heaven as God's Son our Savior. And what we do with that Truth is the most important eternal decision we will ever make. It is not what we do, but what we believe.

JESUS speaking:

I am the good shepherd. I know my own and my own know me and I lay down my life for the sheep. And I have other sheep that are not of this fold. I must bring them also, and they will listen to my voice. So, there will be one flock, one shepherd. (John 10:14-16 ESV)

LINDA MCGREGOR CLARK

O Father give us soft hearts that believe, so we can hear Jesus speaking in the Bible, trust His words and obey and stay on the hard narrow path. Help us to understand that there is only One Shepherd, Who laid down His life for us. Praying in Jesus Christ Name Amen

Jesus was walking in the temple. The Jews then gathered around Him, and were saying to Him, "How long will You keep us in suspense? If You are the Christ, tell us plainly." Jesus answered them, "I told you, and you do not believe; the works that I do in My Father's name, these testify of Me. But you do not believe because you are not of My sheep. My sheep hear My voice, and I know them, and they follow Me; and I give eternal life to them, and they will never perish; and no one will snatch them out of My hand. My Father, who has given them to Me, is greater than all; and no one is able to snatch them out of the Father's hand. I and the Father are one." (John 10:22-30 NASB)

JESUS:

1. Harassed by the Jewish leaders asking Him to tell them He is the Messiah
2. Answered I have told you plainly
3. Leaders did not believe because they were not His sheep
4. Has sheep who hear His voice and follow Jesus
5. Gives eternal life to His sheep
6. No one can snatch us out of His hand
7. Sheep are given to Jesus from His Father
8. He and the Father are one

Remember now how many times Jesus has said that He is God and how many fantastic miracles He has done and how furious the leaders have been! Yet the religious leaders did not like His message, so now Jesus is explaining why some believe and many do not.

O Father, thank You that You and Jesus hold each of the sheep in Your hands and we are secure! Help us to hear Your voice through the verses we are reading and to follow You carefully.

LINDA MCGREGOR CLARK

Just like real sheep, we need our Good Shepherd to bring us back to the flock each time we wander away! Thank You Jesus for being that Good Shepherd! Praying in the Name of the Good Shepherd, Jesus Christ So Be It

---

Jesus said, " I and the Father are One." So, this reaction shows they knew He was saying He is God: the people picked up stones to kill him. Jesus said, "At my Father's direction I have done many good works. For which one are you going to stone me?" They replied, "We're stoning you not for any good work, but for blasphemy! You, a mere man, claim to be God. (John 10:31-36 NLT)

JESUS:

1. Said He and the Father are One
2. Did many good works from the Father
3. Claimed to be God

O Jesus, thank You for being so clear in Your words that we can read them and understand exactly, "You are God the Son, the exact representation of God the Father and once we are in Your hand, no one can snatch us out of Your hand!"
O Holy Spirit continue Your work in our lives to grow our knowledge and understanding of God, and to grow our trust and obedience of Your word in order to convict us when we sin. We need Your help! In Jesus Christ Name Amen

Jesus told her, "I am the resurrection and the life. Anyone who believes in me will live, even after dying. Everyone who lives in me and believes in me will never ever die. Do you believe this, Martha?" "Yes, Lord," she told him. "I have always believed you are the Messiah, the Son of God, the one who has come into the world from God." (John 11:25-27 NLT)

WHO IS JESUS:

1. said He is "I AM", which means He is God
2. is the resurrection and the life, believe in Him and have life everlasting
3. is Messiah (Christ)
4. Son of God
5. came into the world from God.

WHY IS THIS IMPORTANT:

There is salvation in no one else, for there is no other name under heaven given among men by which we must be saved. (Acts 4:12 ESV)

O Holy Spirit help each of us by taking away our blindness to spiritual understanding and give us wisdom from above that is pure, peaceable, gentle, open to reason, full of mercy and good fruits, impartial and sincere. Praying in the name of the Son of God, our only Savior Jesus Christ, So Be It

LINDA MCGREGOR CLARK

Jesus said, "If you trust me, you are trusting not only me, but also God who sent me. For when you see me, you are seeing the one who sent me. I have come as a light to shine in this dark world, so that all who put their trust in me will no longer remain in the dark...But all who reject me and my message will be judged on the day of judgment by the truth I have spoken. I do not speak on my own authority. The Father who sent me has commanded me what to say and how to say it. And I know his commands lead to eternal life; so, I say whatever the Father tells me to say." (John 12:44-50 NLT)

WHO IS JESUS:

1. is fully trustworthy
2. is sent by God
3. is the exact representation of God
4. is The Light to shine in this dark world
5. believe in Him and not be in darkness
6. reject Him and be judged
7. speaks the truth
8. speaks only what The Father tells Him to say
9. tells us that God's commands lead to eternal life.

WHY IS THIS IMPORTANT:

Enter by the narrow gate. For the gate is wide and the way is easy that leads to destruction, and those who enter by it are many. But the gate is narrow, and the way is hard that leads to life, and those who find it are few. (Matthew 7:13-14 ESV)

O Father, all these truths we are reading about Jesus are so important. Please give us complete understanding and hearts that fully believe unto eternal life.

Dear Holy Spirit lead us in the narrow way toward life.

O Jesus we trust in You, continue to lead us in Your truth and teach us You path for You are the God of our salvation. In Jesus Christ name Amen

"Let not your hearts be troubled. Believe in God; believe also in me. Jesus said, "I am the way, and the truth, and the life. No one comes to the Father except through me!" (John 14:1-6 ESV)

JESUS:

1. said we must believe in God and in Him
2. said there is plenty of room in Heaven for those who believe
3. is preparing a special place for each one who believes
4. is coming again to get us and take us to Heaven to be with Him
5. said, " I AM" the Way, the Truth and the Life! No one comes to God except through Me.

WHY IS THIS IMPORTANT:

Jesus said He is the only way to go to the Father and we must go through Him to get to God.

O Father help us to genuinely believe in You and Jesus, so that it effects our hearts and actions and is not just something we think in our minds.

O Jesus, thank You for preparing a special place for each of us and for the promise that You will come back to get us.

O Holy Spirit teach us to cling to the Truth of Jesus's words and to understand that No one gets to heaven except through believing and obeying Jesus. In the Precious Name of Jesus, we pray, Amen

Jesus, although He existed in the form of God (a Spirit), did not regard equality with God a thing to be grasped, but emptied Himself, taking the form of a bondservant, and being made in the likeness of men. Being found in appearance as a man, He humbled Himself by becoming obedient to the point of death, even death on a cross. For this reason also, God highly exalted Him, and bestowed on Him the name which is above every name, so that at the name of Jesus EVERY KNEE WILL BOW, of those who are in heaven and on earth and under the earth, and that every tongue will confess that Jesus Christ is Lord, to the glory of God the Father.
(Philippians 2:6-11 NASB)

WHO IS JESUS:

1. existed in the form of God as a Spirit
2. gave that up
3. emptied Himself and became a slave
4. took the form of a man
5. humbled Himself being obedient to the point of death on the cross
6. God highly exalted Him and gave Him the name which is above ALL names
7. every knee will bow, and every tongue will confess that Jesus is Lord.

WHY IS THIS IMPORTANT:

Jesus said that the work of God was to believe in Him as God the Son, our Savior.

O Holy Lord Jesus, it is hard to imagine what You gave up to come to this earth for the very purpose of suffering and dying for Your enemies, us sinners. It is, also, impossible to express enough thankfulness to You, so we pray for the Holy Spirit

LINDA MCGREGOR CLARK

to help us understand as best we can and fill our hearts with godly praise. We look forward to the time when EVERYONE will know the truth! In Your High and All Powerful Name So Be It

Jesus Christ, the faithful witness, the firstborn from the dead and the ruler of the kings of the earth. To him who loves us and has set us free from our sins by his blood, and made us a kingdom, priests to his God and Father — to him be glory and dominion forever and ever. Amen. Look, he is coming with the clouds, and every eye will see him, even those who pierced him. And all the tribes of the earth will mourn over him. So, it is to be. Amen. "I am the Alpha and the Omega," says the Lord God, "the one who is, who was, and who is to come, the Almighty. A sharp double-edged sword came from his mouth. When I saw him, I fell at his feet like a dead man. He laid his right hand on me and said, "Don't be afraid. I am the First and the Last, and the Living One. I was dead, but look — I am alive forever and ever, and I hold the keys of death and Hades. (Revelation 1:5-18 CSB)

WHO IS JESUS:

1. Christ/Messiah: expected king, deliverer
2. First born from the dead
3. Ruler of the kings of the earth
4. loves His family:
5. Set us free from our sins by His blood
6. made us His kingdom
7. made us priests to God the Father
8. deserves glory and dominion forever
9. Is coming in the clouds
10. everyone will see Him
11. is the Alpha and the Omega
12. is the One who is, who was and is to come
13. is the Almighty
14. is the Son of Man:
15. sharp two-edged sword came out of His mouth
16. is the First and the Last

LINDA MCGREGOR CLARK

17. is the Living One, He died, but is alive forever and ever
18. Holds the key of death and Hades

WHY IS THIS IMPORTANT:

Because Jesus is the only way of salvation, there is absolutely no other way to heaven.

Father help us when we think about Jesus to remember Who He is Now the first born from the dead, the Almighty, The First and the Last and He holds the key to death! Help us to understand that He is God the Son and help us to worship Him properly in Spirit and in Truth. Help us remember that faith in Jesus is the only way to Heaven and eternity with You. According to Your Word So Be It.

Since the most important thing a person will ever do in their life is to have faith in God the Son and in order to have real saving faith, we must believe God's Truth about Jesus, so I want to summarize what we've seen in all the verses about Him:

JESUS:

1. He is the image of the invisible God and exists eternally (not created)
2. created ALL things in heaven and earth
3. ALL things were created through Jesus and for Jesus
4. He is before all things
5. He holds all things together
6. He is the Head of the Church
7. He is the first to be raised from the dead
8. He is preeminent (Sovereign)
9. All the fullness of God lives in Him
10. before He became a man, Jesus existed in the form of God (a Spirit)
11. He gave that up to take the form of a man
12. He humbled Himself to the point of death on the cross
13. God highly exalted Him and gave Him the name above all names
14. the time is coming when every knee will bow and every tongue will confess that Jesus is Lord
15. God speaks to us through Him
16. He is the Heir of all things
17. the world was created through Him
18. He shines with God's glory
19. He has the exact same character as God
20. He sustains the universe by His mighty power
21. He made us pure in God's sight by His sacrifice
22. now He is sitting at God's right hand
23. He is called the Son and God by God the Father
24. His throne endures forever

LINDA MCGREGOR CLARK

25. He rules in justice
26. He is called Lord
27. He laid the foundation of the earth
28. He made the heavens with His hands
29. He is always the same
30. He lives forever
31. He teaches us the Truth
32. He is fully man and fully God
33. He lives in believers through the Holy Spirit
34. He is Head over every ruler and authority.

And to think this Jesus is our Savior from the Wrath of God over our sins!

Worship Him today for Who we have seen He is, by thanking Him for His mercy, grace, and sacrifice. I get excited as I read these lists and realize that the Creator of All things cares about me personally!! My prayer for you is you will be filled with wonder at these awesome TRUTHS, You will believe in Jesus and be saved from God's Wrath against sin and You'll live a life to please the Father God. May it be so.

PROVERBS

❖

These are the proverbs of Solomon, David's son, king of Israel. Their purpose is to teach people wisdom and discipline, to help them understand the insights of the wise. Their purpose is to teach people to live disciplined and successful lives, to help them do what is right, just, and fair. These proverbs will give insight to the simple, knowledge and discernment to the young. (Proverbs 1:1-4 NLT)

Purpose of the Proverbs:

1. teach wisdom and discipline
2. help us be understanding
3. to give instruction in:

   a. wise behavior
   b. Righteousness
   c. justice
   d. fairness

4. insight to the naïve
5. knowledge and discernment

O Father open our eyes of understanding and give us wisdom, knowledge, understanding and discernment as we go through

Your instructions in Proverbs. Give us hearts that desire for us to apply these to our lives and to obey Your rules. In Jesus Christ name Amen

---

The fear of the Lord is the beginning of knowledge; fools despise wisdom and instruction. (Proverbs 1:7 ESV)

O Lord God, our Father, reveal to us Your Infinite Greatness, Holiness and Grace, so we will have profound reverence (fear) of You and will have the beginnings of true knowledge to guide us. Forgive us when we act like fools and go our own way without giving any thought to what would please You. We need Your help! In Jesus Christ name Amen

---

Wisdom calls out if you respond to my warning, then I will pour out my spirit on you and teach you my words....whoever listens to me will live securely and be undisturbed by the dread of danger." (Proverbs 1:20-33 CSB)

O Father give us hearts that listen to wisdom from above and receive the teaching of Your Truth from these Proverbs. Help us to be willing to listen to You and to be quick to learn from Your words. Forgive us when we behave foolishly, then fill us with understanding of Your ways and give us the desire to obey. In Jesus Christ name Amen

LINDA MCGREGOR CLARK

My child listen to what I say and treasure my commands. Tune your ears to wisdom and concentrate on understanding. Cry out for insight and ask for understanding. Search for them as you would for silver; seek them like hidden treasures. Then you will understand what it means to fear the Lord, and you will gain knowledge of God. For the Lord grants wisdom and from His mouth come knowledge and understanding. (Proverbs 2:1-6 NLT)

As a child of God, what am I to do:

1. Listen to God's words
2. Treasure up God's commands
3. Be attentive to wisdom
4. Concentrate on understanding
5. Call out for insight and understanding
6. Search for wisdom like treasure
7. Fear the LORD and gain the knowledge and understanding

Dear Father God, the world is such a wicked place with no fear of God and calling evil good and good evil. We need understanding and wisdom from You! Please Father, protect our hearts and grant us knowledge of You and Your wisdom, so we will fear You and know the Truth. Then we will gain understanding of our God by asking You to help us. Asking in Jesus Christ name So Be It.

The Lord gives wisdom; from his mouth come knowledge and understanding; he stores up sound wisdom for the upright; he is a shield to those who walk in integrity, guarding the paths of justice and watching over the way of his saints. Then you will understand righteousness and justice and equity, every good path; for wisdom will come into your heart, and knowledge will be pleasant to your soul; discretion will watch over you, understanding will guard you, delivering you from the way of evil, from men of perverted speech, who forsake the paths of uprightness to walk in the ways of darkness, (Proverbs 2:6-13 ESV)

LORD:

1. gives wisdom
2. Speaks knowledge and understanding
3. Stores up wisdom for His saints
4. Shields those live in integrity
5. Guards the path of justice
6. Watches over His saints

GOD's FAITHFUL CHILDREN:

1. God gives sound wisdom to us
2. Are upright
3. protected by the Lord
4. understand what is right, just and fair
5. find the right way to go
6. wisdom is in their hearts
7. knowledge of God fills them with joy
8. discerning and understanding to be able to make wise choices
9. will avoid evil people with twisted words, who live in darkness

LINDA MCGREGOR CLARK

Our Father, Almighty God, forgive us for not trying to be pleasing in Your sight and deliver us from every false way. Help us have hearts of wisdom to know You better and to be faithful to You. Help us make wise choices and to avoid even the appearance of wrong by associating with the evil people. According to Your Word, So be it! Amen

---

My child never forget the things I have taught you. Store my commands in your heart. If you do this, you will live many years, and your life will be satisfying. Never let loyalty and kindness leave you! Tie them around your neck as a reminder. Write them deep within your heart. Then you will find favor with both God and people, and you will earn a good reputation. (Proverbs 3:1-4 NLT)

GOD'S CHILDREN:

1. never forget His commands by storing them in their hearts
2. are loyal to Him
3. are kind
4. receive favor from Him
5. have good reputations

Our Father in heaven, give us sharp minds that take in these truths and store them deep within our hearts, so we can be obedient children and always loyal to You. In the name of Your Son, Jesus Christ, our Lord. So be it. Amen

Trust in the Lord with all your heart; do not depend on your own understanding. Seek his will in all you do, and he will show you which path to take. (Proverbs 3:5-6 NLT)

THOUGHTS:

How many times have we heard and even said, "Follow your heart." or "How do you "feel" about...?"! This is from the world's advice, but exactly the opposite of God's word and wisdom.

O Good and Gracious God, Who desires the salvation and then spiritual growth of those whom You called, pour out Your infinite mercies upon us and forgive us when we follow our own hearts instead of seeking Your will in all we do. Help us turn to You, to trust You and to follow You. In Jesus Christ name, So Be It! Amen

Do not be wise in your own eyes; fear the Lord and turn away from evil. This will be healing for your body and strengthening for your bones. (Proverbs 3:7-8 CSB)

GOD'S CHILDREN:

1. Not wise in our own eyes
2. Fear the Lord
3. Turn away from evil

Dear Father God, it is so easy to think we know what is best, forgive us for this and please help us to turn to You, to trust Your wisdom and to turn away from unbelief and evil actions toward living pleasing lives for You. In Jesus Christ name, So Be It.

How blessed is the one who finds wisdom and the one who gains understanding. Wisdom is more precious than jewels; And nothing you desire compares with her. (Proverbs 3:13-15 NASB)

"the wisdom from above is first pure, then peaceable, gentle, open to reason, full of mercy and good fruits, impartial and sincere."(James 3:17 ESV)

WISDOM:

1. blesses the one who finds it and gains understanding
2. profit better than silver
3. gain better than gold
4. more precious than jewels
5. better than anything we can ever want
6. pure
7. peaceable
8. gentle
9. open to reason
10. full of mercy and good fruits
11. impartial and sincere.

O Lord of Wisdom, this is an awfully hard list to follow because we have hearts that are full of our own desires and many times our desires are totally oppsite from Wisdom from above. Forgive us and fill our hearts with Your wisdom from above, so we can have right desires, then live to please You. According to Your Word, So Be It.

Long life is in Wisdom's right hand; In her left hand spiritual riches and honor. Her(wisdom) ways are pleasant ways and all her paths are peace. She(wisdom) is a tree of life to those who take hold of her, and happy are all who hold her tight. (Proverbs 3:16-18 NASB)

Dear Lord give to us fullness of joy, pleasant ways and treasures of peace through Your Wisdom. We need Your help to hold tight to Your Wisdom in this wicked world where most everyone is running down the broad way to destruction! According to Your promise, So Be It.

LINDA MCGREGOR CLARK

The Lord founded the earth by wisdom and established the heavens by understanding. Maintain sound wisdom and discretion my child, do not lose sight of them. They will be life for you and adornment for your neck. Then you will go safely on your way; your foot will not stumble. When you lie down, you will not be afraid; you will lie down, and your sleep will be pleasant. (Proverbs 3:19-24 CSB)

GOD'S CHILDREN:

1. Have sound wisdom and discretion
2. Do not lose sight of wisdom or discernment for they give life
3. Foot will not stumble
4. Lie down and sleep in peace

Our Father fill us with Your wisdom and give us Your understanding, so we will live our lives with discernment and will go safely on our way without stumbling. Thank You for the promise of sweet sleep with no fear. In Jesus Name, So Be It

Do not withhold good from those who deserve it when it's in your power to help them. (Proverbs 3:27 NLT)

Our Father, this world in which we live is full of traps against Your children and we thank You so much for being our security! Fill our hearts with discernment to help us recognize those who are in need and to be quick to help. Also give us generous hearts that are quick to help others who are in need. In Jesus Christ name So Be It

Wisdom is supreme—so get wisdom. And whatever else you get, get understanding. (Proverbs 4:7 CSB)

Dear Father God, we really need godly wisdom and understanding! Teach us Your statues and please fill our hearts and minds with Your wisdom, then we will know Your scripture and we will obey Your rules. So Be It.

I have taught you the way of wisdom; I have led you in the paths of uprightness. When you walk, your step will not be hampered, and if you run, you will not stumble. Keep hold of instruction; do not let go; guard her, for she is your life. (Proverbs 4:11-12 ESV)

GOD'S CHILDREN:

1. Have been taught the way of skillful godly wisdom
2. Have been led in the straight paths of righteousness
3. When you walk, you path will be clear
4. When you run, you will not stumble

O Father God, as Your children, give us listening ears and clear understanding and put Your Spirit within us, so we will be obedient children, who walk Your straight paths through this world. Give us hearts that hold tight to Your instructions and guard Your Truth. Forgive us Father, when we go our own way and walk in the way of the world without a thought of Your will and give us Your Spirit to guide us. In Jesus Christ name So Be It.

LINDA MCGREGOR CLARK

Guard your heart above all else, for it determines the course of your life. (Proverbs 4:23 NLT)

O Jesus, our mouths get us in so much trouble! Help us to be aware that every word we speak is heard by our Heavenly Father. So, we must be diligent to protect our hearts from bad stuff by being very careful what we watch and what we read and to what we listen. Because whatever we put into our hearts will come out of our mouths. It is so easy to lie, forgive us and please Holy Spirit guide us to be honest and truthful, we pray. According to God's Word, So Be It.

Let thine eyes look right on, and let thine eyelids look straight before thee. Turn not to the right hand nor to the left; remove thy foot from evil. (Proverbs 4:25-27 KJV)

THOUGHTS:

This is so important that we are careful with our eyes, because they can cause us to sin by coveting things or people or jobs or talents to name a few desires. So these verses are warning us to be careful and I am reminded of a verse to pray over our eyes, "Turn away mine eyes from beholding vanity (vain, empty, or valueless THINGS) and quicken thou me in thy way." (Psalm 119:37 KJV)

So you can see that God is warning us to be very careful as we are looking around this world because the things of the world can draw us away from God's path which He has set out for us.

O Prayer Hearing, Redeeming Father God, how many distractions that surround us. Forgive us for letting our eyes wander and for not keeping on Your straight and narrow path. Give us eyes that watch our ways and are going straight toward You and away from evil. We need Your help! In the Powerful Name of Christ Jesus, So Be It.

LINDA MCGREGOR CLARK

These six things doth the Lord hate— yea, seven things are an abomination unto him:

- proud look (arrogant),
- a lying tongue,
- hands that shed innocent blood,
- a heart that deviseth wicked imaginations,
- feet that be swift in running to mischief,
- a false witness that speaketh lies,
- he that soweth discord among brethren.

(Proverbs 6:16-19 KJV)

THOUGHTS:

As I look at this list I see our world! Everywhere there is lying in our news, from our leaders, even in the churches. Discord in families seems to be a common situation. We are having riots and destruction all around, plotted by evil prople. Then there is the killing of the innocent babies through abortion. Our only help can come from God!

Holy, holy, holy Father God, we are guilty of so many of these sins and we need Your forgiveness! Open our eyes to see our own sins and give each of us hearts that desire to live lives to please You. Thank You for Jesus, Who made it possible for us to be forgiven and for the Holy Spirit, Who teaches and guides us and makes us more like Jesus every day. We have a long way to grow to be like Jesus, Father, but thank You for Your infinite mercy, love and grace! According to God's Word. So Be It.

My son, keep my words and lay up my commandments with thee. Keep my commandments, and live; and my law as the apple of thine eye. Bind them upon the table of thine heart. Say unto wisdom, Thou art my sister; and call understanding thy kinswomen. (Proverbs 7:1-4 KJV)

THOUGHTS:

In these verses we see several different words used to describe the Bible: Words, Commandments and Law. Next we see what God expects from us toward His words: that we memorize them, we keep(obey) them, and we take the Word as our treasure from which we get wisdom and understanding.The verses show us the importance of God's Word to help us to obey His commands because we love them and have them in our heart.

Our Father in heaven, Your words are True and they are perfect instructions to give us Your wisdom and insight. Help us to make Your Word a beloved part of our lives each day by memorizing Your words and storing them in our hearts. Asking through Jesus Christ Your Beloved Son, So Be It.

LINDA MCGREGOR CLARK

The fear of the LORD is the beginning of wisdom, And the knowledge of the Holy is understanding. (Proverbs 9:10 KJV)

FEAR: deep profound respect and awe of God

THOUGHTS:

Today when I look around our world I see no fear of God, not even in many churches that say they are Christian. We have lost the fear of God because we do not know the God of the Bible, who is holy, holy, holy, who is the Creator of all things, who expects our total worship and obedience, who hates sin so much that He said without the shedding of blood there is no forgiveness, who sees everything we do and knows everything we think and feel, and everything we say. No the God many worship is just there to make us happy and he has no power or authority over us. We must go to God's word to get to know Him and to learn to fear Him, so we will grow in our knowledge and understanding and obedience.

O God Most High, fill our minds and hearts with deep awe and knowledge of You, that will give us wisdom and understanding of the God with Whom one day is like 1000 years and a 1000 years is like a day. Open our eyes to understand You are a Mighty God, Who is Holy, Holy, Holy and Who hates sin, but is quick to forgive us, when we repent of our sins, all because of Jesus' sacrifice.

Oh, the depth of the riches of the wisdom and knowledge of You God! From You and through You and to You are all things. To You be glory forever. Amen

Wise words come from the lips of people with understanding, but those lacking sense will receive punishment. Wise people treasure knowledge, but the babbling of a fool invites disaster. (Proverbs 10:13-14 NLT)

Dear Holy Spirit keep reminding us that we get God's wisdom only from Him through His Word in the bible. So please take these words we read each morning and root them deeply in our hearts, so we will gain the wisdom from above. Give us understanding that treasures God's Wisdom and keep us from being foolish. In Jesus Christ name Amen

LINDA MCGREGOR CLARK

The mouth of the godly person gives wise advice, but the tongue that deceives will be silenced. The lips of the godly speak helpful words, but the mouth of the wicked speaks perverse words. (Proverbs 10:31-32 NLT)

GOD'S CHILDREN:

1. Are godly
2. Give wise advice
3. Speak helpful words

WICKED PEOPLE:

1. Tongue deceives (lies)
2. Speak perverse words (unreasonable, obstinate, contrary)

O Dear Father, we are people of unclean lips and we live in the midst of people with unclean lips! Forgive us and fill our hearts and mouths with wise and helpful words.

O Holy Spirit convict us when we tell lies or use unhelpful words. Remind us that our words must be wise and pleasing to God. Through Christ Jesus our Lord So Be It.

A man who is kind benefits himself, but a cruel man hurts himself....Whoever brings blessings will be blessed, and one who refreshes others will himself be refreshed. (Proverbs 11:17 ESV)

Heavenly Father forgive us, we are selfish people. Please give us self-forgetful spirits, so that we will be more anxious to give to others than to receive gifts, more eager to help others, then to be helped, more thoughtful of others and less mindful of ourselves. In Jesus Christ name So Be It.

A hard worker has plenty of food, but a person who chases fantasies has no sense. Wise words bring many benefits, and hard work brings rewards. (Proverbs 12:11,14 NLT)

Heavenly Father, thank You for the book of Proverbs! There is so much Wisdom in these verses. Give us understanding, so we will learn Your rules and obey them with all our hearts. Help us to think before we speak, then speak wisely and to always be diligent, hard workers and not lazy people. For Your glory, So Be It.

LINDA MCGREGOR CLARK

The way of a fool is right in his own eyes, but a wise man listens to advice. (Proverbs 12:15 ESV)

We live in a society of fools, everyone is "following their own heart!" But God's Word to us says:
The heart is deceitful above all things, and desperately sick; who can understand it? (Jeremiah 17:9 ESV)

O Wise and Forgiving Father God, we have been fools and even said or thought "I need to follow my heart!" Forgive us for only thinking about ourselves and not listening to You through Your Word and through godly advice from others. Give us wisdom to understand the difference between bad and good advice, and between good and the Best advice. We need Your help!! Asking through the name of Jesus Christ. So Be It.

Truthful words stand the test of time but lies are soon exposed....The Lord detests lying lips, but he delights in those who tell the truth. (Proverbs 12:19 NLT)

O mercy, Father, here is another sin we so easily do! We tell "little white lies" or exaggerate when telling about events or just outright lie, because we are insecure or selfish and well, everyone else does it. Forgive us, fill us with truth and help us to live lives of truth that please You. In Jesus Christ name Amen

The one who has contempt for instruction will pay the penalty, but the one who respects a command will be rewarded. (Proverbs 13:13 CSB)

Teach us Lord, to love instruction and to respect Your commands. Teach us when to be silent and when to speak; when to act or not to act, so that in our daily lives, we will do Your will on earth as it is in heaven. In Jesus Name Amen

---

Whoever walks with the wise becomes wise, but the companion of fools will suffer harm. (Proverbs 13:20 ESV)

O Most Wise Father, You have said if we want wisdom all we need to do is pray and ask You, then You will give it to us. Now we read that we must, also, be sure our friends are wise, because we become like the people with whom we spend time. Give us understanding and discernment so we will recognize whether our friends are wise or foolish, then draw us closer to the wise. In the Powerful Name of Jesus Christ So Be It

LINDA MCGREGOR CLARK

Whoever lives with integrity fears the Lord, but the one who is devious in his ways despises the Lord. (Proverbs 14:2 CSB)

Our Pure and Holy Lord show us our devious ways and forgive us when we participate in ways that You hate. Fill our hearts with Truth and integrity. Dear Jesus, thank You for rescuing us from our slavery to sin and making it possible to fear God and desire to please Him. So Be It, Amen

There is a way that seems right to a man, but its end is the way to death. (Proverbs 14:12 ESV)

In those days there was no king in Israel. Everyone did what was right in his own eyes. (Judges 21:25 ESV)

**This is the culture in which we live**:

1. follow your own heart
2. do what you think is right
3. take care of yourself first
4. love yourself

All doing what is right in our own eyes.

**But God's Word says just the opposite**:

"The human heart is the most deceitful of all things, and desperately wicked. Who really knows how bad it is? But I, the Lord, search all hearts and examine secret motives. I give all people their due rewards, according to what their actions deserve." (Jeremiah 17:9-10 NLT)

O Holy Spirit save us from our own hearts and teach us the Truth from God's Word! Do not let us live according to the culture but help us understand that God's ways are exactly the opposite! We need Your help as we've each said and believed these very sayings. Cleanse our hearts and fill them with The Truth, according to our Father God. In King Jesus our Savior's Name Amen

LINDA MCGREGOR CLARK

The backslider in heart will have his fill of his own ways, but a good man will be satisfied with his. The naive believes everything, But the sensible man considers his steps.
(Proverbs 14:14-15 NASB)

O Lord God, another reminder from You to us that we must be wise and carefully consider our way of life! Forgive us when we go our own way and thank You for reminding us not to follow our own heart, but to get to know You better and to live only to please You. We need Your help, Holy Spirit!! Praying according to Your wisdom and Truth. So Be It

One who is wise is cautious and turns away from evil, but a fool is reckless and careless.
(Proverbs 14:16 ESV)

O Holy Spirit, You're living in the hearts of God's children to guide us and help us to understand The Truth and to grow to be more like Jesus every day and The Father has said in His Word that when we ask for wisdom, He will give it abundantly. So, we are asking for the wisdom to live very cautiously and to recognize things or people or entertainment or anything else that is reckless and careless, so we will stay away from them. O Father forgive us whenever we are foolish for there are many times when we plunge ahead and need You to rescue us. Thank You for being patient with Your children. In the Savior's Name, So Be It

In the fear of the LORD there is strong confidence, And His children will have a place of refuge. The fear of the LORD is a fountain of life, to turn one away from the snares of death. (Proverbs 14:26-27 NKJV)

THOUGHTS:

Fear of God results in being careful to please God by avoiding things that offend the Holy God. One way to know when we are offending God is to check if what we're doing needs to be hidden from anyone.

Dear Father, help us to know and understand You better, so we will learn exactly the things that please You and recognize if our actions are offensive to You or pleasing to You. Help us live pure lives in Your presence, which is everywhere. In Jesus Christ name Amen

---

Gentle words turn away wrath, but harsh words stir up anger. (Proverbs 15:1 NASB)

Our Gracious and Gentle Lord Jesus, we see how important words are, as we look at Your life. Your words were always true and just what the hearers needed. But we live in a world of very harsh words and lots of anger, so our words, many times, are just blurted out and not helpful. Forgive us and fill us Lord with Your love, making our words true and gentle. Praying in Your Name So Be It.

LINDA MCGREGOR CLARK

The tongue of the wise makes knowledge appealing, but the mouth of a fool spews out foolishness. (Proverbs 15:2 NLT)

O Dear Father, another warning about our words which we speak! Help us remember that our words reflect what is in our hearts. Fill our hearts with Your love, so our words will not be foolishness, but will be wise and gentle. For Jesus's sake, So Be It.

The eyes of the Lord are in every place, keeping watch on the evil and the good. (Proverbs 15:3 ESV)

O Father as You are watching over our lives give us hearts that do good and keep us from evil. Help us to do Your will on earth as it is in heaven, in order to please You and bring You Glory. Because of Jesus our Savior So Be It

A gentle tongue is a tree of life, but perverseness in it breaks the spirit....The lips of the wise spread knowledge; not so the hearts of fools. (Proverbs 15:4 & 7 ESV)

__Perverseness__: corrupt, obstinate, deliberate and stubborn unruliness, rebellious.

O Father God forgive us when we let perverseness control our tongues and do not use them to spread gentleness, wisdom and Truth. Set a guard at the door of our lips, so we may speak only that which pleases You. Help us realize that the things we put into our hearts and hear with our ears, are the things which come out of our lips. Praying through Jesus Christ, Your Son Amen

LINDA MCGREGOR CLARK

Better is a little with the fear of the LORD than great treasure and trouble with it. Better is a dinner of herbs where love is than a fattened ox and hatred with it. (Proverbs 15:16-17 ESV)

**Fear of the LORD**: profound reverence and awe, which results in obedience.

The fear of the LORD is the beginning of wisdom; all those who practice it have a good understanding! (Psalms 111:10 ESV)

Holy Holy Holy are You, our Father! Fill us with reverence and awe of You, as we go through this day. Make us aware that our very breath is a gift from Your hand of grace! Fill our minds with awe at the thought of the God of the Universe, Who holds everything together, has come to us in infinite love to save us from His wrath! Forgive us LORD for our indifference and fill us with Your wisdom. So Be It

He whose ear listens to the life-giving correction will dwell among the wise. He who neglects discipline despises himself, but he who listens to reproof acquires understanding. (Proverbs 15:31-32 NASB)

Dear Father God give us ears that are quick to listen to correction and forgive us for the many times we neglect discipline. Surround us with wise, godly people, who will give us the Truth and fill us with understanding! In Your Son Jesus's Name So Be It

The fear of the Lord is what wisdom teaches, and humility comes before honor.
(Proverbs 15:33 CSB)

Fear: profound reverence and awe toward God

Almighty Sovereign Creator God, our Father, Your Word tells us, over and over, that we are to fear in order to understand You and to be wise. But we focus on You making us happy by giving us things, instead of wanting to be obedient children or to be humble. So, Father, please forgive us for simply wanting You to bless our plans and desires. Help us to know You better as we read Your word, to understand You better and to genuinely love You, so we will fear and obey You. In Jesus Christ name Amen

He who gives attention to the word will find good. And blessed is he who trusts in the LORD.
(Proverbs 16:20 NASB)

Our Father, thank You for Your book, the Bible, which is Your words of wisdom, given to us to reveal Yourself to Your children! Give us listening ears and hearts that trust You with Your plan and Design for our lives, then we will understand Your word and trust in You. In Jesus Christ name Amen

LINDA MCGREGOR CLARK

There is a way which seems right to a man, but its end is the way of death. (Proverbs 16:25 NKJV)

Jesus said to him, "I am the way, and the truth, and the life; no one comes to the Father but through Me. (John 14:6 NASB)

In those days...everyone did what was right in his own eyes. (Judges 21:25 ESV)

Holy Father, thank You that You have made the narrow way to heaven a clear way thru Jesus. But we live in a time when everyone does what they think sounds right and they take the easy way. Forgive us for trying to get to heaven by the many easy ways that sound good to us, instead of carefully following the only, narrow way. Give us hearts that desire Your narrow way, only through Jesus! In His Name we pray Amen

"Whoever is slow to anger is better than the mighty, and he who rules his spirit than he who takes a city."(Proverbs 16:32 ESV)

O Father being slow to anger and ruling our spirits are hard things, because we are so selfish and impatient. Forgive us of quick tempers, help us to do justice, to love mercy and to live humbly before You. In Jesus Christ name Amen

The one who is lazy in his work is brother to a vandal.
(Proverbs 18:9 CSB)

O Father we have all been lazy at one time or another, but we have never thought of laziness as being the same as a person who vandalizes! Please forgive us and help us to be quick to do our work from now on. In Jesus Christ our Savior's Name, So Be It.

Wise words satisfy like a good meal; the right words bring satisfaction. The tongue can bring death or life; those who love to talk will reap the consequences. (Proverbs 18:20-21 NLT)

Father, wise words will be pure, peaceable, gentle, open to reason, full of mercy and good fruit, impartial and sincere. Please help us to think before we speak, so that the consequences of our words will be pleasing to You and to us and will bring life to others. In Jesus Christ name So Be It.

LINDA MCGREGOR CLARK

Whoever gets wisdom loves his own soul; he who keeps understanding will discover good. (Proverbs 19:8 ESV)

O Father, Your Proverb tells us to get wisdom and wisdom comes from You, so we are asking You to fill us with Your wisdom from above. Also understanding comes from You, therefore we need You in our life to help us to be wise obedient children. Give us hearts that love Your law. In Christ Jesus name Amen

Listen to advice and accept instruction, that you may gain wisdom in the future. (Proverbs 19:20 ESV)

Oh Lord, Your hands have made and fashioned us; give us understanding that We may learn your commandments and gain wisdom and understanding. According to Your word So Be It.

If you stop listening to correction, my child, you will stray from the words of knowledge. (Proverbs 19:27 CSB)

O Lord help us keep our way pure, By guarding it according to your word. With our whole heart Help us seek you; let us not wander from your commandments! And put the desire to store your word in our heart, that we might not sin against you. Praying according to Your word, So Be It

Wine is a mocker, strong drink a brawler, and whoever is led astray by them is not wise.
(Proverbs 20:1 ESV)

Dear Father, how important Your words are to us, so we can get understanding and learn to hate what You hate. Forever O Lord, Your word is settled in heaven! Make our hearts sound in Your statues, so we may not be ashamed and not be led astray by strong drinks. We need Your wisdom to guide us. In the Lord and Savior's name, Amen

---

Who can say, "I have kept my heart pure; I am clean and without sin"? (Proverbs 20:9 NIV)

If we say we have no sin, we deceive ourselves, and the truth is not in us. If we confess our sins, he is faithful and just to forgive us our sins and to cleanse us from all unrighteousness. If we say we have not sinned, we make him a liar, and his word is not in us. (1 John 1:8-10 ESV)

O Father, we are surrounded by much wickedness and that makes us sometimes think we are pretty good, when compared to others. But we need to compare ourselves to the things that make You happy. Help us to see our own sins, so we can repent, be forgiven and cleansed of our unrighteousness. Through the blood of Jesus Christ Amen.

LINDA MCGREGOR CLARK

Every way of a man is right in his own eyes, but the Lord weighs the heart. To do righteousness and justice is more acceptable to the Lord than sacrifice. (Proverbs 21:2-3 ESV)

"I the Lord search the heart and test the mind, to give every man according to his ways, according to the fruit of his deeds." (Jeremiah 17:10 ESV)

O Wise, Righteous Judge of all, our Father, we are not righteous, and we need Your help! We just live without any thought of what would please You. Forgive us Father. Fill us with the desire to be acceptable to You by doing the righteous works which You have prepared for us to do. So Be It.

Whoever pursues righteousness and kindness will find life, righteousness, and honor.
(Proverbs 21:21 ESV)

<u>*RIGHTEOUSNESS*</u>: means a person that is trustworthy, acting in accord with God's law

O Father, we have an awfully long way to go to be righteous. But give us hearts that desire to pursue righteousness and kindness, so our lives will please You. For Jesus's sake, Amen.

Listen closely, pay attention to the words of the wise, and apply your mind to my knowledge. For it is pleasing if you keep them within you and if they are constantly on your lips. (Proverbs 22:17-18 CSB)

THOUGHTS:

Remember Wise words are pure, peaceful, gentle, open to reason, full of mercy and good fruits, impartial and sincere. So, these are the words to which we are to pay attention.

Oh Lord Jesus, our Savior and King, it will be difficult to hear these kinds of words since we're bombarded with mostly unwise words. Give us ears that recognize wisdom and help us pay attention and even speak wisely. Praying in Your name, So Be It.

Apply your heart to instruction and your ear to words of knowledge. (Proverbs 23:12 ESV)

Dear God, the Holy Spirit, You are our Teacher sent from God the Father to instruct us in the ways of pleasing the Father through our obedience. Open our ears to knowledge of the Truth and give us hearts that love instruction in God's Word. According to the word So Be It.

LINDA MCGREGOR CLARK

I walked by the field of a lazy person, the vineyard of one with no common sense. I saw that it was overgrown with nettles. It was covered with weeds, and its walls were broken down. Then, as I looked and thought about it, I learned this lesson:

A little extra sleep, a little more slumber, a little folding of the hands to rest—then poverty will pounce on you like a bandit; scarcity will attack you like an armed robber.
(Proverbs 24:30-34 NLT)

THOUGHTS:

This is true when there is neglect of anything for which we are responsible: school, work, our home and yard, our bodies, to name a few. I am sure you can think of other things we neglect. But the most important thing is we should never be spiritually lazy for that will produce thorns and weeds in our hearts and minds.

"Only be on your guard and diligently watch yourselves,
(Deuteronomy 4:9 CSB)

Gracious Father God open our eyes that we may see wonderful things from Your word. Give us understanding so we will be diligent to watch ourselves and guard our hearts. Make us fully aware of the importance of always being diligent. Asking through Jesus Christ, Your Son, our Savior. So Be It.

A word fitly spoken is like apples of gold in a setting of silver. (Proverbs 25:11 ESV)

THOUGHTS:

There is power in our words and to speak just the right words at the right time can strengthen weak faith or can give guidance or encouragement.

Dear Wise Gracious Father, we need to be aware of the importance of all our words and to think before we speak. So that our words will be like golden apples. Forgive us for just blurting out insensitive words! Praying in the Savior's name Amen

We have been reading selected verses in Proverbs because these verses will help us grow more mature.

Proverbs was written to:

1. teach wisdom and discipline
2. Help us understand wise words
3. To give instructions in:

    a. wise behavior
    b. Righteousness
    c. good behavior
    d. fairness

4. Give insight to the naive
5. Teach knowledge and discernment
6. Teach us the Fear of the LORD and the need for wisdom

Proverbs also shows us who a child of God is:

1. listens to God's Words
2. Treasures up God's commands
3. attentive to wisdom
4. Calls out for discernment and understanding
5. Fears the LORD and grows in the knowledge of God
6. Never forgets His commands by storing them in their hearts
7. Are loyal to God
8. Are kind
9. Have good reputations
10. Trust in God with all their hearts
11. Guard their hearts above all else
12. Are generous
13. speak words of encouragement
14. are not lazy
15. are obedient

This is a noticeably short summary of what we've read in Proverbs. My prayer for each of us is that we will remember these and do our best to live lives pleasing to God. Also, I pray we will be diligent to guard our hearts from darkness. May it be so.

LINDA MCGREGOR CLARK

PSALMS

❖

Oh, the joys of those who do not follow the advice of the wicked, or stand around with sinners, or join in with mockers. But they delight in the law of the Lord, meditating on it day and night. They are like trees planted along the riverbank, bearing fruit each season. Their leaves never wither, and they prosper in all they do. But not the wicked! They are like worthless chaff, scattered by the wind. They will be condemned at the time of judgment. Sinners will have no place among the godly. For the Lord watches over the path of the godly, but the path of the wicked leads to destruction.
(Psalm 1:1-6 NLT)

O Father God fill us with delight in Your Word and help us to realize that You are watching over our paths as we meditate on Your Word. Make our lives fruitful with the fruit of the Holy Spirit: love, joy, peace, patience, kindness, goodness, faithfulness, gentleness, self-control and prayer. In Jesus Christ name Amen

This Psalm was written about 1000 years before Jesus came to earth, but it is a prophecy about Him:

Why do the nations rage and the peoples plot in vain? The kings of the earth take their stand, and the rulers conspire together against the Lord and his Anointed One: "Let's tear off their chains and throw their ropes off of us." The one enthroned in heaven laughs; the Lord ridicules them. Then he speaks to them in his anger and terrifies them in his wrath: "I have installed my king on Zion, my holy mountain." I will declare the Lord's decree. He said to me, "You are my Son; today I have become your Father. Ask of me, and I will make the nations your inheritance and the ends of the earth your possession. You will break them with an iron scepter; you will shatter them like pottery." So now, kings, be wise; receive instruction, you judges of the earth. Serve the Lord with reverential awe and rejoice with trembling. Pay homage to the Son or he will be angry and you will perish in your rebellion, for his anger may ignite at any moment. All who take refuge in him are happy.
(Psalms 2:1-12 CSB)

O Father help us understand these verses that clearly show us You and Jesus. Forgive us when we rebel and desire to do things our own way. Cause us to serve You in reverence, to take refuge in Jesus and to be thankful. Thank You, Thank You, Thank You for sending Jesus to be the LORD of lords and KING of kings, our SAVIOR!! In Jesus Christ name Amen

LINDA MCGREGOR CLARK

Give ear to my words, O Lord; consider my groaning. Give attention to the sound of my cry, my King and my God, for to you do I pray. O Lord, in the morning you hear my voice....let all who take refuge in you rejoice; let them ever sing for joy, and spread your protection over them, that those who love your name may exult in you. For you bless the righteous, O Lord; you cover him with favor as with a shield. (Psalms 5:1-12 ESV)

O Lord, You are our King and our God, and we do pray to You each morning. As we set forth into this new day, we take refuge in You. Fill us this day with joyful praise. In Jesus Christ name Amen

---

O Lord, our Lord, how majestic is your name in all the earth! You have set your glory above the heavens....When I look at your heavens, the work of your fingers, the moon and the stars, which you have set in place, what is man that you are mindful of us and the son of man that you care for me? Yet you have made us a little lower than the heavenly beings and crowned us with glory and honor. You have given us dominion over the works of your hands; O Lord, our Lord, how majestic is your name in all the earth! (Psalms 8:1-9 ESV)

WOW God! You not only created us and gave us this wonderful place in which to live, but when we rebelled against You, then You sent Jesus to make it possible for us to be forgiven and to call You Father! Help us to see Your majestic name all around and to live lives in Awe of You Alone. Make us thankful children, Father, who love and worship You and are obedient. In Jesus Christ name Amen

I will give thanks to the Lord with my whole heart; I will recount all of your wonderful deeds. I will be glad and exult in you; I will sing praise to your name, O Most High....But the Lord sits enthroned forever; he has established his throne for justice, and he judges the world with righteousness; he judges the peoples with uprightness. The Lord is a stronghold for the oppressed, a stronghold in times of trouble. And those who know your name put their trust in you, for you, O Lord, have not forsaken those who seek you. Sing praises to the Lord, who sits enthroned in Zion(Heaven)! (Psalms 9:1-2,7-11 ESV)

O Father, it is so good to be reminded that You are on Your throne and in times of stress and trouble we can totally trust You! Create in us hearts of praise, thankfulness and trust for Your deeds in our lives. In the Holy name of Jesus Christ Amen

---

Pneumonia is no fun, so My prayer for me this morning and anyone else who is feeling sick and overwhelmed and cannot say a prayer but want to pray. You may use a Psalm as your prayer:

How long, O LORD? Will You forget me forever? How long will You hide Your face from me? How long shall I take counsel in my soul, Having sorrow in my heart all the day? How long will my enemy(sickness) be exalted over me? Consider and answer me, O LORD my God; Enlighten my eyes, or I will sleep the sleep of death, And my enemy will say, "I have overcome him(her)," But I have trusted in Your lovingkindness; My heart shall rejoice in Your salvation. I will sing to the LORD, Because He has dealt bountifully with me. (PSALM 13:1-6 NASB)

LINDA MCGREGOR CLARK

Preserve me, O God, for in you I take refuge. I say to the Lord, "You are my Lord; I have no good apart from you."...The Lord is my chosen portion and my cup; you hold my lot....I bless the Lord who gives me counsel; in the night also my heart instructs me. I have set the Lord always before me; because he is at my right hand, I shall not be shaken....You make known to me the path of life; in your presence there is fullness of joy; at your right hand are pleasures forevermore. (Psalms 16:1-11 ESV)

O Father God, please fill us with peace, strong faith and complete trust in Your Providence, as we settle back into life's daily routines. Comfort us and make known to us Your presence and help us run to You for refuge, so we will not be shaken. And remind us often that You love us!! IN THE MIGHTY NAME OF JESUS CHRIST AMEN

I call upon you, for you will answer me, O God; incline your ear to me; hear my words. Wondrously show your steadfast love, O Savior of those who seek refuge...at your right hand. Keep me as the apple of your eye; hide me in the shadow of your wings,...As for me, I shall behold your face in righteousness; when I awake, I shall be satisfied with your likeness. (Psalms 17:6-8, 15 ESV)

O Father God, we call on You in thankfulness for hearing our prayers. Now, give us hearts that recognize Your face all around us, make us satisfied with You and give us ears to listen to the Holy Spirit as He guides us. In Jesus Christ name Amen

I love you, O Lord, my strength. The Lord is my rock and my fortress and my deliverer, my God, my rock, in whom I take refuge, my shield, and the horn of my salvation, my stronghold. I call upon the Lord, who is worthy to be praised, and I am saved from my enemies....In my distress I called upon the Lord; to my God I cried for help. From his temple he heard my voice, and my cry to him reached his ears....For it is you who light my lamp; the Lord my God lightens my darkness....This God—his way is perfect; the word of the Lord proves true; he is a shield for all those who take refuge in him. (Psalms 18:1-6, 28-30 ESV)

THE LORD MY GOD:

1. My strength
2. My rock
3. My fortress
4. My deliverer
5. My refuge
6. My shield
7. My salvation
8. My stronghold
9. Is worthy to be praised
10. Saves me from my enemies
11. Hears my cries
12. My light in darkness
13. Perfect
14. Word is true

O Father, what a wonderful description of You as our Strength, our Rock, our Fortress, our Deliverer, our Shield, our Salvation and our Stronghold!! Keep these names of Yours in our heart, so when we get distressed, we will immediately call on You, because You always hear our voice and answer. Thank You that we can trust Your perfect way and be sure Your Word is True. You are worthy of praise! We pray in the name of Jesus Christ Amen

LINDA MCGREGOR CLARK

For who is God, but the Lord? And who is a rock, except our God?—the God who equips me with strength and makes my way blameless. He made my feet like the feet of a deer and set me secure on the heights....You have given me the shield of your salvation, and your right hand supports me,...You gave a wide place for my steps under me, and my feet did not slip....The Lord lives, and blessed be my rock, and exalted be the God of my salvation—For this I will praise you, O Lord, among the nations, and sing to your name. (Psalm 18:31-46 ESV)

O Father, thank You for the words of this Psalm that we can fully embrace! Thank You for equipping us with Your strength and for giving us a wide place on which to walk, that is secure. We praise You for being the God of our salvation!! Fill our hearts with faith to believe You always have our way in Your control and are making us fit for heaven. In Jesus Christ name Amen

The heavens declare the glory of God, and the sky above proclaims his handiwork. (Psalms 19:1 ESV)

THOUGHTS:

This is a short verse but says so much! In fact, every time I see a sunset or sunrise I think of this verse. Because sunsets and sunrises definitely proclaim God's handiwork. I have, also, begun to notice the beautiful colors and designs of the different birds which God created. They proclaim God's handiwork too. Just remember when you are awed by the mountains, the clouds, the flowers, our own bodies, anything that was created by our God is shouting, "God is my Creator!"

O Father, thank You for this reminder that You make each day to declare Your glory and to remind us that You are in control. It is hard to see Your handiwork when we are grumbling about the weather and we need Your forgiveness and help from the Holy Spirit to see Your glory and handiwork each day. Thank You for loving us and for patiently teaching us to depend on and trust in You. In Jesus Christ name Amen

LINDA MCGREGOR CLARK

The instructions of the Lord are perfect, reviving the soul. The decrees of the Lord are trustworthy, making wise the simple. The commandments of the Lord are right, bringing joy to the heart. The commands of the Lord are clear, giving insight for living. Reverence for the Lord is pure, lasting forever. The laws of the Lord are true; each one is fair. They are more desirable than gold, even the finest gold. They are sweeter than honey, even honey dripping from the comb. They are a warning to your servant, a great reward for those who obey them. (Psalms 19:7-11 NLT)

GOD'S WORD:

1. Perfect instructions that revive the soul
2. Trustworthy decrees that make the simple wise
3. Commandments that are right and bring joy to the heart
4. Commands are clear and give insight
5. Laws are True and fair
6. More desirable than gold and sweeter than honey
7. Are warnings
8. Great reward for those who obey

O Father, these verses are reminding us that Your Word, the whole bible, which is filled with Your instructions, decrees, commandments and laws are all perfect and true, and our obedience of them brings joy to us and causes us to be in awe of our God. Help us to love Your Guide for our life and to be obedient to Your Commandments. In Jesus Christ name Amen

How can I know all the sins lurking in my heart? Cleanse me from these hidden faults. Keep your servant from deliberate sins! Do not let them control me. Then I will be free of guilt and innocent of great sin. (Psalms 19:12-13 NLT)

O Father, You have charged us to keep your commandments carefully. Oh, that our actions would consistently reflect your decrees! Then we will not be ashamed when we compare our lives with your commands. As we learn your righteous laws, we will thank you by living as we should! We will obey your decrees. Please do not give up on us! In Jesus Christ Holy Name Amen

Let the words of my mouth and the meditation of my heart be acceptable in your sight, O Lord, my rock and my redeemer. (Psalms 19:14 ESV)

O Holy Spirit fill our hearts with the things that are pleasing to our Heavenly Father, so when we speak, the words coming from our mouths will be acceptable to You and a blessing to those around us. Help us remember that whatever we say comes from what is in our hearts, so we need to fill our hearts with God acceptable, lovely things. In Jesus Christ name may it be so.

LINDA MCGREGOR CLARK

May the Lord answer you in the day of trouble! May the name of our God protect you! May he send you help from the church and give you support from Heaven! (Psalms 20:1-2 ESV)

O Father, it is so wonderful to know that as Your children, we can call on You when we need help, because of Jesus's perfect life, sacrifice and resurrection, You hear us and send us help! We are very needy children, Father. But You are infinitely able to help and always know exactly what we need. Thank You, Thank You, Thank You! In Jesus Christ name Amen

May our God grant your heart's desires and make all your plans succeed. May we shout for joy when we hear of your victory and raise a victory banner in the name of our God. May the Lord answer all your prayers....Some boast of their chariots and horses, but we boast in the name of the Lord our God. (Psalms 20:4-5 NLT)

O Father, we do have some heart's desires and we make lots of plans, but today we are just asking that You fill us with total trust in Your plans for our lives. Help us to boast in Your name because You are the Lord our God. In the Loving, Powerful Name of Jesus Christ Amen

For the we trust in the Lord, and through the steadfast love of the Most High we shall not be moved....Be exalted, O Lord, in your strength! We will sing and praise your power. (Psalms 21:7, 13 ESV)

O Father, we are so glad You are our Most High God, Who is completely trustworthy and loves His children with steadfast love. Help us keep these truths with us and to remember we can always trust You. So Be It.

The Lord is my shepherd; I shall not want. He makes me lie down in green pastures. He leads me beside still waters. He restores my soul. He leads me in paths of righteousness for his name's sake. Even though I walk through the valley of the shadow of death, I will fear no evil, for you are with me; your rod and your staff, they comfort me. You prepare a table before me in the presence of my enemies; you anoint my head with oil; my cup overflows. Surely goodness and mercy shall follow me all the days of my life, and I shall dwell in the house of the Lord forever. (Psalms 23:1-6 ESV)

THOUGHTS:

This Psalm is a perfect description of our relationship with God the Son Jesus, who is our Shepherd. Sheep are not very smart and need a good shepherd to lead them and to protect them from themselves and from enemies. Sheep have poor eyesight but have good hearing and follow the Shepherd. They are timid, quiet, gentle and obedient. Well, obviously we do not have all these qualities but it is interesting to see how God could call us sheep who need a Good Shepherd. May we follow our Good Shepherd and know He will walk with us through our lives and protect us.

O Father, what a special Psalm You have given us to use in times of sorrow. Help us to remember that You are always our Shepherd, who guides us in safe paths that take us ultimately directly to Heaven. Thank You for grace and forgiveness and most of all for Jesus Christ, our Savior and Lord. Praying in His name may it be so.

The earth is the Lord's, and everything in it. The world and all its people belong to him. For he laid the earth's foundation on the seas and built it on the ocean depths. Who may climb the mountain of the Lord? Who may stand in his holy place? Only those whose hands and hearts are pure, who do not worship idols and never tell lies. They will receive the Lord's blessing and have a right relationship with God their savior. Such people may seek you and worship in your presence, O God...(Psalms 24:1-6 NLT)

GOD'S CHILDREN:

1. Belong to God, along with the whole world
2. Hands and hearts are pure
3. Do not worship idols
4. Never tell lies
5. Receive God's blessing
6. Have a right relationship with God their Savior
7. Will seek God and worship in His presence

O God Most High and Holy, Creator of the whole earth, Governor of the universe, Judge of all people, Savior of sinners; thank You for making it possible for us to seek You and worship You because of Jesus's sacrifice that paid for our sins!! Forgive us when we love other things more than You and when we tell lies. Make our hands and hearts pure through Jesus's blood. We pray in the wonderful name of the Savior Jesus Christ Amen

LINDA MCGREGOR CLARK

Lift up your heads, O gates, And be lifted up, O ancient doors, That the King of glory may come in! Who is the King of glory? The LORD strong and mighty, The LORD mighty in battle. Lift up your heads, O gates, And lift them up, O ancient doors, That the King of glory may come in! Who is this King of glory? The LORD of hosts, He is the King of glory. (Psalm 24:7-10 NASB)

WHO IS THE LORD:

1. The King of glory
2. The LORD Strong and Mighty, mighty in battle
3. The LORD of Hosts

O Father, what a wonderful, mighty reminder of Who You are! You are the King of glory, strong and mighty, LORD of all and worthy of praise and worship! And to think that You would love us, who are everything completely opposite of You and make us part of Your family. This brings us to our knees in repentance and thankfulness! We worship things like money, family, friends, success, and popularity; forgetting that each of these come from You as gifts to us to use for Your glory. Thank You, Jesus for Your blood that paid the terrible price for our wicked sins!! In Your Holy Name So Be It.

O Lord, I give my life to you. I trust in you, my God! Show me the right path, O Lord; point out the road for me to follow. Lead me by your truth and teach me, for you are the God who saves me. All day long I put my hope in you. (Psalm 25:1-5 NLT)

GOD'S CHILDREN:

1. Give our lives to Him
2. Trust our God to show us the right path
3. God leads us by His truth and teaches us
4. God saves us
5. Hope in God

O Father, we do give our lives to You and trust in You! Thank You for being the God of our Salvation! We need You to show us the narrow road to follow as we learn Your Truth in the Bible. Help us to put our complete hope in You as we go through this day. In Jesus Christ name Amen

Remember, Lord, your compassion and your faithful love, for they have existed from eternity. Do not remember the sins of my youth or my acts of rebellion; but in keeping with your faithful love, remember me because of your goodness, Lord. (Psalms 25:6-7 CSB)

O Lord our Lord, we need Your compassion and always faithful love because we are sinners. Thank You Jesus for Your faithful love and goodness that makes it possible for God to forgive us and not remember our many sins. To God be Glory forever Amen

LINDA MCGREGOR CLARK

Good and upright is the Lord; therefore he instructs sinners in the way. He leads the humble in what is right, and teaches the humble his way. (Psalms 25:8-9 ESV)

O Father You are Good and You always do what is right! Thank You for showing us the proper way to live as Your children. Forgive us when we are proud and go our own way, which is often, and give us hearts that listen to Your teaching us Your ways. In Jesus Christ name Amen

The Lord leads with unfailing love and faithfulness all who keep his covenant and obey his demands. For the honor of your name, O Lord, forgive my many, many sins. (Psalm 25:10-11 NLT)

O God, we know You are still on Your throne and You do lead Your children with strong never-ending love and You are always faithful to us! The sacrifice of Jesus and His blood covering Your children, Father, is so important because we still need Your forgiveness for our many, many sins. Thank You Father God, Savior Jesus, Holy Spirit our Guide and Counselor! Amen

Who is the man who fears the Lord? Him will the Lord instruct in the way that he should choose. His soul shall abide in well-being...The friendship of the Lord is for those who fear him, and he makes known to them his covenant. (Psalms 25:12-14 ESV)

FEAR is deep awe and respect of God that produces a life that desires to please God in everything we do, say, think or feel.

Dearest Lord, help us to really understand what it means when Your Bible says we are to fear You, since there are so many verses that repeat the message that we are to fear You and You promise to teach us and to reveal Your ways to us as we fear You, then we need Your help to understand and to really fear You in a way that is pleasing to You. We pray in Jesus Christ Holy Name Amen

My eyes are continually toward the LORD, For He will pluck my feet out of the net. (Psalms 25:15 NASB)

O LORD God, You are our Preserver, Governor, Savior and Rescuer. Help us to remember that our help comes from You. Help us to be watchful over our ways and diligent to watch over our hearts. Make us aware of our sins and quick to turn to You for rescue through our repentance. Thank You for all Your grace! In Jesus Christ name Amen

LINDA MCGREGOR CLARK

O LORD Turn to me and be gracious to me, for I am lonely and afflicted. The troubles of my heart are enlarged; bring me out of my distresses. Consider my affliction and my trouble, and forgive all my sins....Oh, guard my soul, and deliver me! Let me not be put to shame, for I take refuge in you, my God. (Psalms 25:16-20 ESV)

O Father, these verses are perfect for our family in this time with the loss of our son, brother, husband, dad, nephew, uncle, and cousin, Darrell. We are lonely and distressed but we are taking refuge in You, please give us stronger faith, guard our souls and deliver us from our loneliness. In Jesus Christ name Amen

The Lord is my light and my salvation— so why should I be afraid? The Lord is my fortress, protecting me from danger, so why should I tremble? (Psalm 27:1 NLT)

O LORD, this is one of the many Psalms that King David wrote, we thank You for filling him with Your Holy Spirit and enabling him to put even our thoughts and feelings into words. Teach us to hold onto these truths that You are our Light for our paths and our Salvation, our Fortress for protection and we have nothing to fear! It is hard sometimes not to worry (fear), forgive us again and grow our faith! In Jesus Christ name Amen

One thing have I asked of the Lord, that will I seek after: that I may dwell in the house of the Lord all the days of my life, to gaze upon the beauty of the Lord and to inquire in his temple. For he will hide me in his shelter in the day of trouble; he will conceal me under the cover of his tent; he will lift me high upon a rock. (Psalms 27:4-5 ESV)

Our Father in heaven, what a wonderful way to live, always aware of Your presence and knowing that You are close. Help us to learn to trust Your protection in our days of trouble and give us eyes to see Your hand in our lives. In the Most Powerful Name of the Savior Jesus Christ So Be It.

Hear me as I pray, O Lord. Be merciful and answer me! My heart has heard you say, "Come and talk with me." And my heart responds, " Lord, I am coming."...Teach me how to live, O Lord. Lead me along the right path...(Psalms 27:7-8, 10 NLT)

O Lord, we do need Your mercy everyday and we thank You so much that we can come to You, tell You our desires and You always hear our cries! Continue to teach us how You want us to live and give us ears to hear You leading us along the narrow path to eternity in heaven. In Jesus Christ name Amen

　LINDA MCGREGOR CLARK

I am confident I will see the Lord's goodness while I am here in the land of the living. Wait patiently for the Lord. Be brave and courageous. Yes, wait patiently for the Lord. (Psalm 27:13-14 NLT)

O LORD, thank You that we can have faith that we will see Your goodness in our lives. Give us the ability to be brave and courageous and unafraid because we are sure You are always with us working in our lives for Your glory and our growth in faith. Praying in Jesus Christ name Amen

Blessed be the Lord, for he has heard the sound of my pleading. The Lord is my strength and my shield; my heart trusts in him, and I am helped. Therefore my heart celebrates, and I give thanks to him with my song. The Lord is the strength of his people; he is a stronghold of salvation for his anointed. (Psalms 28:6-8 CSB)

O Father, what a wonderful promise that You hear our prayers and give us strength to survive these times. Help us remember that You are our strength and our shield, then give us trusting, thankful hearts that sing our thanks to You for our salvation. In the Powerful Name of Jesus, So Be It

Honor the Lord...honor the Lord for his glory and strength. Honor the Lord for the glory of his name. Worship the Lord in the splendor of his holiness...The Lord rules overall. The Lord reigns as king forever. The Lord gives his people strength. The Lord blesses them with peace.

(Psalms 29:1-2,10-11 NLT)

THE LORD:

1. Is to be honored for His glory and strength
2. Honor Him for the glory of His name
3. Worship Him in holiness
4. Rules over all
5. Reigns as King forever
6. Gives strength to His people and blesses them with peace

O Father, You are very Great, the Maker and Sustainer of all things and we honor You for the Glorious Splendor of Your Holiness! We are so glad You are our Father and that You give us strength to survive and You bless us with peace in our busy busy lives. Remind us daily of these wonderful truths! In Jesus Christ name, may it be so.

LINDA MCGREGOR CLARK

Sing praise to the LORD, you His godly ones, And give thanks to His holy name. For His anger is but for a moment, His favor is for a lifetime; Weeping may last for the night, But a shout of joy comes in the morning. (Psalms 30:4-5 NASB)

THOUGHTS:

In the Bible, God's children are called: His godly ones, saints, faithful ones, chosen, sons, righteous, heirs and many other wonderful names to help us understand who we are in the eyes of God, because of Jesus's sacrifice for our many sins. Therefore, we can praise our Heavenly Father with shouts of joy!!!

O Father, we do sing praises to You and give thanks to You for Your love, mercy and forgiveness! Thank You that our weeping only lasts a short time, but joy is eternal! Fill our hearts and mouths with thanksgiving to You. In Jesus Christ name Amen

Oh, how abundant is your goodness, which you have stored up for those who fear you and worked for those who take refuge in you, in the sight of the children of mankind!...Blessed be the Lord, for he has wondrously shown his steadfast love to me...I had said in my alarm, "I am cut off from your sight." But you heard the voice of my pleas for mercy when I cried to you for help. Love the Lord, all you his saints! The Lord preserves the faithful but abundantly repays the one who acts in pride. Be strong, and let your heart take courage, all you who wait for the Lord! (Psalm 31:19,21-24 ESV)

THE LORD:

1. His abundant goodness is stored up for those who fear Him
2. Works for those who take refuge in Him
3. Wondrously shows His steadfast love for His children
4. Hears our pleas for mercy
5. Preserves the faithful
6. Abundantly repays the arrogant

HIS SAINTS:

1. Fear the Lord
2. Take refuge in the Lord
3. Is loved steadfastly by the Lord
4. Cry to the Lord for help
5. Are heard by the Lord
6. Love the Lord
7. Are Faithful and preserved by the Lord
8. Are strong and courageous and wait for the Lord

O Father, more wonderful truth about Your "steadfast love" to us and our tendency to forget, as we cry and feel like we are cut off from Your sight. Help us Lord to be courageous and fill

LINDA MCGREGOR CLARK

us with love, faith and patience as we wait for You. Thank You for Your goodness, for our protection and for always working in our lives to bring Yourself glory and to give us what is best for our souls. In Jesus Christ name Amen

---

Oh, what joy for those whose disobedience is forgiven, whose sin is put out of sight! Yes, what joy for those whose record the Lord has cleared of guilt, whose lives are lived in complete honesty! Finally, I confessed all my sins to you and stopped trying to hide my guilt. I said to myself, "I will confess my rebellion to the Lord." And you forgave me! All my guilt is gone. Therefore, let all the godly pray to you while there is still time, that they may not drown in the floodwaters of judgment. (Psalm 32:1-6 NLT)

THOUGHTS:

WOW what a beautiful description of the joy of being forgiven. Our disobedience is forgiven and actually put out of God's sight. Because of Jesus our record of sins is cleared and we are no longer guilty.

O Father, thank You, thank you, thank You for mercy, grace and forgiveness through Jesus Christ! So that when we confess our many sins, You are quick to respond and take away our guilty conscience. Thank You that the blood of Jesus has paid the penalty for our judgement and as Your children, we can have joy instead of sadness. Fill us with Your love, thankfulness and real repentance. So Be It.

You are my hiding place; You preserve me from trouble; You surround me with songs of deliverance. (Psalm 32:7 NASB)

THOUGHTS:

What a wonderful promise! God is our place to hide from trouble! When I am feeling sad because someone I know is sick or injured or I have had a deep loss, I will surround myself with all kinds of gospel music to help me hold onto to my Father God, and you know what...It helps!!

O Father God, Thank You for being our place to run to for help in our troubles and for wonderful songs of faith to which we can listen and be comforted. Fill us with faith and trust in You. In Jesus Christ Powerful Name Amen

The Lord says, "I will guide you along the best pathway for your life. I will advise you and watch over you. Do not be like a senseless horse or mule that needs a bit and bridle to keep it under control." (Psalm 32:8-9 NLT)

THOUGHTS:

David is telling us that the Lord will guide us in the pathway He has for our life. He will take good care of us and does not want us to behave like an animal who must have a bit and bridle to make them go in the right direction.

O Father Who hears our prayers, we need Your guidance to find the best way for our lives. Thank You that You have given us the Bible, the Holy Spirit and godly teachers to show us what You want for us and that these tools will lead us in God's narrow way. Also keep us always obedient to what Your Word says first of all. Protect us from the lies of the world and fill us with the Wisdom from above. In Jesus most precious name Amen

Many are the sorrows of the wicked, but steadfast love surrounds the one who trusts in the Lord. Be glad in the Lord, and rejoice, O righteous, and shout for joy, all you upright in heart! (Psalm 32:10-11 ESV)

THOUGHTS:

In this Psalm of David, we see him praising God for His steadfast love that surrounds everyone who trusts in the Lord God. David is rejoicing and excited about God's love and wants everyone who is God's child (the Righteous) to praise God with him with shouts of joy.

Our Father in heaven, it always amazes us that when You look at Your servants, You refer to us as righteous and upright in heart, because our hearts are not even close to being so! Yet Jesus has covered our hearts with His blood, and we have forgiveness and are surrounded by Your unchanging love as we learn to trust You in our lives. Help us to grow in the joy of trust as we are quick to repent and look to You. In the name of Jesus, the Savior Amen

---

Rejoice in the LORD, O you righteous! For praise from the upright is beautiful. (Psalm 33:1 NKJV)

O LORD, we do rejoice in You and we praise You for Your word that is right and true! Give us hearts full of joyful songs to You for You do everything perfectly! Also give us hearts that trust You fully even when we do not understand Your plan, because Your Word is True! In Jesus Christ name Amen

LINDA MCGREGOR CLARK

The word of the Lord holds true, and we can trust everything he does. He loves whatever is just and good; the unfailing love of the Lord fills the earth. The Lord merely spoke, and the heavens were created. He breathed the word, and all the stars were born. (Psalm 33:4-6 NLT)

THE LORD:

1. His word is True
2. Can be trusted in all things
3. Loves righteousness and justice
4. His lovingkindness fills the earth
5. By His word the heavens were created, and the stars were born

O Father, Your Word is True and we can trust every word of the Bible. You are the Creator of all things and You hold the universe together by Your power! We can depend on You because whatever You do is righteous and good. Fill our hearts with faith to believe and obey. In the name of God the Son, Jesus Christ So Be It

I sought the Lord, and he answered me and delivered me from all my fears. Those who look to him are radiant, and their faces shall never be ashamed. This poor person cried, and the Lord heard me and saved me out of all my troubles. The angel of the Lord encamps around those who fear him and delivers them. (Psalm 34:4-7 ESV)

THOUGHTS:

These verses and actually almost the whole Psalm 34 are a very special comfort for God's children who are hurting because of a terrible lose of someone who was loved deeply. I pray that each reader of this devotional who, also, needs to be helped and comforted by our God will receive that comfort as you read this Psalm in the same way as the writer was helped when we lost our son.

O Father, the last few months have been hard for our family. We are crying out for help, for comfort and for wisdom. Your word says You hear our cries and save us out of all our troubles, we ask for this! We need Your deliverance from our fears and troubles and sadness. Fill the whole family with Your peace and comfort. Praying in the Powerful Loving Name of Jesus Christ Amen

LINDA MCGREGOR CLARK

Oh, taste and see that the Lord is good! Blessed is the man who takes refuge in him!...The eyes of the Lord are toward the righteous and his ears toward their cry...When the righteous cry for help, the Lord hears and delivers them out of all their troubles. (Psalm 34:8,15,17 ESV)

O LORD, thank You for the promise that You see us and hear us when we seek You and take refuge in You and cry out for help. Thank You for delivering us out of all our troubles. Help us to remember to turn to You when things are hard or painful and then to trust You to take care of us especially when we do not understand Your plans. In Jesus Christ name Amen

---

The Lord is near to the brokenhearted and saves the crushed in spirit. Many are the afflictions of the righteous, but the Lord delivers him out of them all....The Lord redeems the life of his servants; none of those who take refuge in him will be condemned. (Psalm 34:18-19,24 ESV)

O Father, thank You so much that You are always near us to save us from our painful sorrows and to deliver us out of them all. Help us to quickly take refuge in You and to trust Your plan for our lives, even when we do not understand!

Oh, the depth of the riches and wisdom and knowledge of You God! How unsearchable are Your judgments and how inscrutable Your ways! For who has known the mind of the Lord, or who has been Your counselor? Or who has given a gift to You that You would have to repay him? For from You and through You and to You are all things. To You be glory forever! Amen.

Lord, your faithful love reaches to heaven, your faithfulness to the clouds. Your righteousness is like the highest mountains, your judgments like the deepest sea. Spread your faithful love over those who know you, and your righteousness over the upright in heart. (Psalm 36:5-10 CSB)

O Father God, the Author of all good, we thank You so much for Your faithfulness, love, righteousness and perfect judgements toward Your children! Thank You that we can take refuge in You and be refreshed. Give us hearts that trust You in all circumstances and eyes to see Your Light in this dark world. In Jesus Christ name Amen

I have been young and now I am old, Yet I have not seen the righteous forsaken Or his descendants begging bread... Wait for the LORD and keep His way, the salvation of the righteous is from the LORD; He is their strength in time of trouble. He delivers them and saves them, Because they take refuge in Him. (Psalm 37:23-40 ESV)

THOUGHTS:

Our God promises that He will not forsake any of His children or any of our descendants and we can trust every one of His promises because He has always kept all of His promises and as soon as we take refuge in Him He will deliver us and save us.

O Father teach us to take refuge in You. Show us Your salvation and hold our hands! Send Your comfort that is perfect and give us peace as we learn to trust You. In Jesus name Amen

LINDA MCGREGOR CLARK

I waited patiently for the Lord; he inclined to me and heard my cry. He drew me up from the pit of destruction, out of the miry bog, and set my feet upon a rock, making my steps secure. He put a new song in my mouth, a song of praise to our God! (Psalm 40:1-3 ESV)

THOUGHTS:

Patiently waiting is not easy in this rush rush world. We live with instant gratification in everything from food to games to school to life. Therefore the Holy Spirit must instill in our hearts and minds the patience we need to be content and trusting in waiting for the Lord.

O Father, these verses are so encouraging. Thank You for giving us a solid place on which to stand! Give us hearts that trust Your promises and help us to live our lives following Your Truth. O Holy Spirit, there are so many voices around us, give us discernment to recognize the Truth or a lie and boldness to stand up for Truth. In Jesus Christ name Amen

Let all who seek You rejoice and be glad in You; Let those who love Your salvation say continually, "The LORD be magnified!" Since I am afflicted and needy, Let the Lord be mindful of me. You are my help and my deliverer; Do not delay, O my God. (Psalm 40:16-17 NASB)

THOUGHTS:

What wonderful qualities spoken of our God: He causes us to rejoice and be glad in Him, He gives us salvation, He is magnificent, He knows us, helps us, and is our deliverer! What a incredible Father God we have!

O Father, at times we feel afflicted and needy, but we thank You that we are always in Your thoughts! Help us to quickly turn to You for our help, so we can say "Glory to God!" and really mean it from our hearts because we trust You fully. In Jesus Christ name Amen

LINDA MCGREGOR CLARK

As the deer pants for the water brooks, So my soul pants for You, O God. My soul thirsts for God, for the living God; (PSALM 42:1-2a NASB)

O Father God give us these types of souls, that have deep longing for You. Souls that want to know and understand You and desire to live lives which are pleasing to You. Forgive us for living as if You do not exist and for desiring other things or other people, instead of You. Bring back to our minds Your wonderful names that will draw us closer to You and fill our souls with the proper longings. Through the excellence of Christ Jesus, Your dear and only Son, our Savior. So Be It

Reader, I went through these very feelings off and on yesterday. But I remembered God Who is always present loving, teaching, guiding and giving mercy and forgiveness, whenever we turn back to Him!

Why are you in despair, O my soul? And why have you become disturbed within me? Hope in God, for I shall again praise Him For the help of His presence. O my God, my soul is in despair within me; Therefore I remember You.(PSALM 42:5-6 NASB)

Heavenly Father, we do allow ourselves to become disturbed and to despair. But thank You that when we "remember You", You are the God Who is Always There! Forgive us for our wondering hearts and please Holy Spirit keep our LORD ever before us. Asking through Jesus Christ, Your Son, our Savior. So Be It

But each day the Lord pours his unfailing love upon me, and through each night I sing his songs, praying to God who gives me life....Why am I discouraged? Why is my heart so sad? I will put my hope in God! I will praise him again— my Savior and my God! (Psalm 42:8 & 11 NLT)

THOUGHTS;

It is good to read and understand in God's Word that there are always other people who have the same feelings, worries and sorrows, which we have. And they get comfort when they put their hope in God, praise Him and are thankful in all things!

O Lord, Who never leaves imperfect those in whom You have begun a good work, even though we still sin and get discouraged, grant that we may repent, be forgiven and be thankful for Your unfailing love toward Your children. Give us souls that sing of Your Faithfulness and that hope in You. In the name of Your Son Jesus Christ our Lord and Savior So Be It.

LINDA MCGREGOR CLARK

Send out your light and your truth; let them lead me; let them bring me to your holy hill and to your dwelling! Then I will go to the altar of God, to God my exceeding joy, and I will praise you with music, O God, my God. (Psalm 43:3-4 ESV)

O God, our Father God, Your Light and Truth are The Bible and Jesus is the Light of the world so as we read small sections of it in our devotions, cause them to lead us to You and fill us with exceeding joy and thankfulness. Then we will worship You properly and grow in understanding and obedience. In the name of Jesus Christ Amen

Clap your hands, all peoples! Shout to God with loud songs of joy! For the LORD, the Most High, is to be feared. For God is the King of all the earth; sing praises with a psalm! God reigns over the nations; God sits on his holy throne. For the shields of the earth belong to God; he is highly exalted! (Psalm 47:9 ESV)

THOUGHTS:

LORD written with all uppercase always means "I AM", the name God gave to Moses, when Moses asked God His Name. So whenever you are reading the Bible and see LORD written in all uppercase then you know that name is God's personal name. Also, this should be a warning to each of us not to use God's name in vain!

LORD, THE GREAT SUSTAINER OF ALL THINGS, we acknowledge that all things come from You — life, breath, sight, touch, goodness, Truth and beauty — everything which makes our existence possible. Help us remember that without You we are dead, because You are the MOST HIGH GOD, King over all the earth! Fill our minds today with thoughts of thankfulness that THE GREAT I AM is in absolute control and You are our Father, if we believe in Jesus Christ, the Savior of the chosen. So Be It

LINDA MCGREGOR CLARK

We have thought on Your lovingkindness, O God, In the midst of Your temple. As is Your name, O God, So is Your praise to the ends of the earth; Your right hand is full of righteousness. For such is God, Our God forever and ever; He will guide us until death. (PSALM 48:9-14 NASB)

O God, Only Wise and Good, our Father, make us remember Your unfailing love and to praise You in the sanctuary or wherever we find ourselves. Keep us aware that You are guiding Your children at all times, even till we die, showing us how greatly You love us and that You expect us to repent of our sins and to obey. Through Your well-beloved Son Jesus Christ. So Be It

We have thought on Your lovingkindness, O God, In the midst of Your temple. As is Your name, O God, So is Your praise to the ends of the earth; Your right hand is full of righteousness. For such is God, Our God forever and ever; He will guide us until death. (PSALM 48:9-14 NASB)

GOD:

1. Faithful love
2. Name is known to the ends of the earth
3. Many people praise Him
4. Full of righteousness and justice
5. Is eternal
6. Guides His people until we die

O God, Only Wise and Good, our Father, make us remember Your unfailing love and to praise You wherever we find ourselves. Keep us aware that You are guiding Your children at all times, even till we die, showing us how greatly You love us and expect us to repent and obey. Through Your well-beloved Son Jesus Christ. So Be It

LINDA MCGREGOR CLARK

May our God come and not keep silence; Fire devours before Him, And it is very tempestuous around Him. He summons the heavens above, And the earth, to judge His people...And the heavens declare His righteousness, For God Himself is judge. "Hear, O My people, and I will speak; I am God, your God. For every beast of the forest is Mine, The cattle on a thousand hills. I know every bird of the mountains, And everything that moves in the field is Mine. If I were hungry, I would not tell you, For the world is Mine, and all it contains. Call upon Me in the day of trouble; I shall rescue you, and you will honor Me." (PSALM 50:7-15 NASB)

THOUGHTS:

What an Almighty Powerful God is pictured here: He is not silent in His approach, fire consumes everything in front of Him and a powerful storm surrounds Him, the heavens declare that He judges in righteousness. Everything on earth and in the earth belongs to God and this God will rescue us and we will honor Him!

O Judge of all the Universe, The Just and Righteous, our Father, because of Your mercy and forgiveness we honor You! These verses remind us that You are Immense, and we are Not! Forgive us for living as if we are god of our own world and use these verses to convict us of our need of Jesus to intercede for us and stand in our place when You judge us. For from You and through You and to You are all things! To God Be the Glory! So Be It

Be gracious to me, God, according to your faithful love; according to your abundant compassion, blot out my rebellion. Completely wash away my guilt and cleanse me from my sin. For I am conscious of my rebellion, and my sin is always before me. Against you—you alone—I have sinned and done this evil in your sight. So you are right when you pass sentence; you are blameless when you judge. Surely you desire integrity in the inner self, and you teach me wisdom deep within. Purify me with hyssop, and I will be clean; wash me, and I will be whiter than snow. (Psalm 51:1-7 CSB)

THOUGHTS:

This Psalm of David was written by him when Nathan the prophet came to see David and confronted him about his immorality with Bathsheba and then his murder of her husband to try to cover up his sin. This is a beautiful picture of what it means to repent, especiality when David says "Against You and You only have I have sinned and done evil in Your sight!" My prayer for you and for myself is that we will see our sin so clearly that we will understand how serious it is to sin against God and how thankful we should be for Jesus! O LORD HELP US!

Holy Holy Holy LORD God of Hosts, the One Who hates sin and Judges in Righteousness! Like David in these verses, teach us to be aware of our many sins against You and fill us with integrity and wisdom then wash us clean from our wickedness. So, we will be whiter then snow through Your Son Jesus, our Savior. So Be It

LINDA MCGREGOR CLARK

Create in me a clean heart, O God, And renew a steadfast spirit within me. Do not cast me away from Your presence And do not take Your Holy Spirit from me. Restore to me the joy of Your salvation And sustain me with a willing spirit
(PSALM 51:10-12 NASB)

Most Merciful and Forgiving Father, Who hates sin and iniquities, these words from You are a wonderful prayer for Your children to repeat. Since we constantly need our own sins blotted out, our hearts cleaned, and our joy restored. Renew our spirits within us and make us willing to repent and obey. In Your Son's name, So Be It.

The sacrifices of God are a broken spirit; A broken and a contrite(sorrowful) heart, O God, You will not despise.
(PSALM 51:17 NASB)

O Father of all mercy, we are sinful children and we need to have broken hearts over our sins. Yet we just try to do "better" instead of really repenting. Forgive us for our hard hearts and give us the desire to really repent and to please You with proper praise. Through Jesus Christ our Savior, Amen

I trust in the lovingkindness of God forever and ever. I will give You thanks forever, because You have done it, And I will wait on Your name, for it is good. (PSALM 52:8-9 NASB)

O Father God, we live in a world of many people who have no interest in You and who think their possessions are enough to keep them safe. Also, almost everyone speaks evil about others and then try to destroy others by their lying,and destructive words. But Father, fill us with the knowledge of Your holiness and make us dependent on You for our refuge, as we trust in Your lovingkindness and protection. Also, Father forgive our words that we speak, which are not good or helpful and fill our mouths with words that please You. According to the purpose of the cross, So Be It.

LINDA MCGREGOR CLARK

This I know that God is for me. In God I trust; I shall not be afraid. What can man do to me? O God; I will render thank offerings to you. For you have delivered my soul from death, yes, my feet from falling, that I may walk before God in the light of life. (Psalm 56:9-13 ESV)

GOD'S CHILDREN:

1. God is for us
2. Trust in God and shall not be afraid
3. Give thanks to God
4. Souls are delivered from death
5. Our feet are on solid ground
6. Live before God in the Light

O LORD our God, thank You that Your Word is for Your children and that You have delivered Your children from death through the Light of Life, Your Son Jesus. Make our hearts to trust and obey You. Fill us with thankfulness and praise to You, so that our feet will not fall, and we will live our lives always aware of Your presence. Through the blood of the Light of the World, Jesus Christ, So Be It.

Be merciful to me, O God, be merciful to me, for in you my soul takes refuge; in the shadow of your wings I will take refuge, till the storms of destruction pass by. I cry out to God Most High, to God who fulfills his purpose for me. He will send from heaven and save me; God will send out his steadfast love and his faithfulness! (Psalm 57:1-3 ESV)

Thoughts:

What a wonderful prayer asking God for mercy and taking refuge in Him when life is full of storms. Trusting in the Most High God and knowing that He will complete His purpose for us and finally save us and send us to heaven!

O Father, the God of Mercy, Who fulfills His purpose for His children, thank You that we can cry out to You and take refuge in You, then You will send Your steadfast love and faithfulness to save us and bring us comfort during storms and dangers in our lives. Keep us in Your Word, so these truths will ever remind us of Your promises and give us hearts full of faith to believe. In Jesus Christ name Amen

I will give thanks to you, O Lord, among the peoples; I will sing praises to you among the nations. For your steadfast love is great to the heavens, your faithfulness to the clouds. Be exalted, O God, above the heavens! Let your glory be over all the earth! (Psalm 57:9-11 ESV)

O Dear Father, Who's constant, faithful love is the Greatest and Who is forever faithful in Your plan for our lives, fill our minds with real faith in You, so that we will bring glory to You and exalt You this day! Forgive us for grumbling and complaining, worrying and forgetting the Truth in these verses. Please fill our hearts with Your praises, which we will share with those around us and let others see we are Your thankful children. Because of Jesus, So Be It!

As for me, each morning I will sing with joy about your unfailing love. For you have been my refuge, a place of safety when I am in distress. O my Strength, to you I sing praises, for you, O God, are my refuge, the God who shows me unfailing love. (Psalm 59:16-17 NLT)

Dear Father God, Your Power and Steadfast Love are the place to which we can run for safety in our times of distress. You are our Strength and Refuge, help our souls to rejoice and sing Your praises in every circumstance of our lives. Forgive us when we get all worked up with worry or anger or frustration or sorrow and forget to turn to You and trust You for peace. Thank You for Your Love and Forgiveness that never ever change, because You are The Unchangeable Lord of All! We pray according to Your Promises in Your Word through Jesus Christ may it be so.

Hear my cry, O God, listen to my prayer; from the end of the earth I call to you when my heart is faint. Lead me to the Rock that is higher than I, for you have been my refuge, a strong tower against the enemy. Let me dwell in your tent forever! Let me take refuge under the shelter of your wings! (Psalm 61:1-4 ESV)

O God, our Rock, Strong Tower and Refuge! Thank You that You hear the cry of Your children and deliver us from all our fears. There is a day of rest coming soon when Your children will live forever in Your heaven and always in Your presence! Lead us there through the narrow gate, by Jesus the Lamb that was slain Asking in Jesus Christ's name, may it be so.

LINDA MCGREGOR CLARK

I wait quietly before God, for my victory comes from him. He alone is my rock and my salvation, my fortress where I will never be shaken....Let all that I am wait quietly before God, for my hope is in him. He alone is my rock and my salvation, my fortress where I will not be shaken. My victory and honor come from God alone. He is my refuge, a rock where no enemy can reach me. O my people, trust in him at all times. Pour out your heart to him, for God is our refuge. (Psalm 62:1-2,5-8 NLT)

THOUGHTS:

This Psalm is an example of using God's words to pray according to His will and being sure that He hears your prayer. You can use these verses for a perfect prayer! As you read them, apply them to yourself:

O my Father help me to wait quietly before You for I know that my victory comes from You. You alone are my rock and my salvation, my fortress where I will never be shaken. Let all that I am wait quietly before You my God, because my hope is in You. You alone are my rock and my salvation, my fortress where I will not be shaken. My victory and honor come from You my God, alone. You are my refuge, a rock where no enemy can reach me. Father help me trust in You at all times. I am pouring out my heart to You, my Heavenly Father for You are my refuge. According to Your Word, So Be It!

O God, You are my God; I shall seek You earnestly; My soul thirsts for You, my flesh yearns for You, In a dry and weary land where there is no water. (PSALM 63:1 NASB)

O God, we live in a world that cannot satisfy! We are always looking for a new experience or wanting a new toy. We really need souls that yearn for You, and thirst for You, Dear Father. Forgive our worldly hearts and fill us with heavenly desires that look to You for our satisfaction, because of Christ Jesus, our Savior, Who died to take away our sins and rose to give us new lives which hunger and thirst for God. So Be It.

LINDA MCGREGOR CLARK

Because Your steadfast love is better than life, My lips will praise You. So, I will bless You as long as I live; I will lift up my hands in Your name. When I remember You on my bed, I meditate on You in the night watches, For You have been my help, And in the shadow of Your wings I sing for joy. My soul clings to You; Your right hand upholds me. (PSALM 63:3-4,6-8 NASB)

THOUGHTS:

Learning to praise our God for our whole lives can be an adventure, because if you are like me, my first reaction to waking up in the middle of the night is to complain not praise or meditate. So in reading these verses, I believe we need to remember all the wonderful times when God has held us tight and comforted us by the Holy Spirit, showing us His faithful love in our times of trouble. Also, I have memorized some special verses (Romans 11:33-36) that remind me that God is rich in wisdom and we will never completely understand Him but we are just to remember He is God and we are not. Therefore, sing praises no matter what you are feeling because God knows best.

Because, Father, You never fail to love Your children, please give us understanding to be able to praise You endlessly, even when You say "no" to our prayers or we are sad or we are sick and slow to heal. Sometimes we cannot sleep, or we awaken in the night; at those times, help us remember that You are always there to protect Your children, just like a Mother bird will take her chicks under her wings. O Father help us cling to You and thank You for holding us tight! According to Your Word So Be It.

Ｈow blessed is the one whom You choose and bring near to You To dwell in Your courts (PSALM 65:4 NASB)

O God of our salvation, Who is Mighty and Sovereign, if we are Your children, then we are blessed to have been chosen, to be brought near to You and to live in Your presence forever! Grant that we always keep in mind this impossible to calculate benefit and that we will be ever dependent on Your Power and Goodness, So we will always be ready to give praise to You, through Jesus Christ, Your Son So Be It.

Ｍy flesh and my heart may fail, but God is the strength of my heart and my portion forever. (Psalm 73:26 ESV)

THOUGHTS:

This world in which we are living, in the year 2020, is an absolute mess! There are riots occuring in several large cities in the USA and even around the world. In some of the western states of our country the fires are burning up thousands of acres of forest along with the towns. Yet I am so thankful that God is where I get my strength even though my flesh and my heart may be failing, He is mine, my Father, my Savior, my Protector, Whose love will never fail me.

O our LORD God, our strength and our portion, it is good to be near You when things in this world on which we have depended are failing, like our bodies or possessions or people we love. Thank You for being our refuge and fill hearts with faith and our lips with praise for Your Sovereignty over all and Your Unfailing Love for Your children. In Your Son's Name So Be It.

LINDA MCGREGOR CLARK

Blessed are those who dwell in your house, ever singing your praise! Blessed are those whose strength is in you, in whose heart are the highways to Zion. For a day in your courts is better than a thousand elsewhere. I would rather be a doorkeeper in the house of my God than dwell in the tents of wickedness. O LORD of hosts blessed is the one who trusts in you! (Psalm 84:4-12 ESV)

ZION is another name for heaven.

O LORD God of hosts hear our prayer; give ear, O God! The LORD of All, Who gives favor and honor to those who live upright lives, we need deeper trust in You and a longing for heaven instead of setting our hearts on the temporary things of this world. The description in these verses is wonderful, but most of the time this is not for what our hearts are longing. Forgive us and change our hearts, so we really do desire to be in Heaven with You. Please O LORD So Be It.

Teach me your way, O Lord, that I may walk in your truth; unite my heart to fear your name. I give thanks to you, O Lord my God, with my whole heart, and I will glorify your name forever. For great is your steadfast love toward me; you have delivered my soul from the depths of Sheol.
(Psalm 86:11-13 ESV)

GOD'S SERVANT:

1. Taught by God
2. Walks in His truth
3. Fears His name
4. Thankful heart
5. Glorifies God forever
6. Steadfastly loved by God
7. Delivered from hell

O Lord our God teach us to trust Your ways and to live in Your Truth. Great is Your steadfast love toward us and You are constantly at work in our lives to deliver us from evil. You are the only real relief of those who put their trust in You, continue to draw us closer and fill us with Your praise. In the name of Your Dear Son, Jesus, our Savior So Be It

LINDA MCGREGOR CLARK

O Lord God of Heaven's Armies! Where is there anyone as mighty as you, O Lord? You are entirely faithful. The heavens are yours, and the earth is yours; everything in the world is yours—you created it all. Righteousness and justice are the foundation of your throne. (Psalm 89:8-14 NLT)

O God, the Only Wise and Good God, Who never stops showing to Your children how greatly You love and favor them, especially when You gave us a King and Savior, Jesus Christ, Your only Son, we ask that You give us the grace to be obedient to Him and be repentant each time we sin by our disobedience. Fill us with the praise that we just read in this Psalm and remind us throughout today of Your Majesty, Power and Faithfulness. So Be It.

This I declare about the LORD: He alone is my refuge, my place of safety; he is my God, and I trust him. He will cover me with his feathers. He will shelter me with his wings. His faithful promises are my armor and protection. The LORD says, "I will rescue those who love me. I will protect those who trust in my name. When they call on me, I will answer; I will be with them in trouble. (Psalm 91:2-15 NLT)

O Father God Most High, The Almighty, give us the faith to cling to You in times of trouble and to know You alone are our refuge. Thank You for another example of a Mother bird with her wings spread out over her chicks as a picture of Your love and protection of Your children! We need lots of reminders of Who You are! Forgive us for forgetting that You have promised to answer Your children when we call on You and to protect us, all because of Your only Son, our Savior Jesus Christ. Amen

L ORD, I will shout for joy because of the works of your hands. How magnificent are your works, LORD though the wicked sprout like grass and all evildoers flourish, they will be eternally destroyed. But you, LORD, are exalted forever. The righteous thrive like a palm tree and grow like a cedar tree in Lebanon. They will still bear fruit in old age, healthy and green, to declare: "The LORD is just; he is my rock, and there is no unrighteousness in him." (Psalm 92:4-15 CSB)

THOUGHTS:

What a promise, "I will still bear fruit in old age!" Now that I am a Great Grandmother to four and Grandmother to eight, it is reassuring to have my God say that I will bear healthy fruit even now! So I have a promise that this little book will produce some fruit for the LORD, who will say "The LORD is my rock." Okay Father, I believe and look forward to the results.

You, O LORD are loving and faithful and Your works are wonderful! You are exalted and in Justice You punish the wicked, but the righteous will thrive even as we grow old. According to Your promises, So Be It.

LINDA MCGREGOR CLARK

The LORD reigns, he is robed in majesty; Your throne was established long ago; you are from all eternity. Mightier than the thunder of the great waters, mightier than the breakers of the sea— the LORD on high is mighty. Your statutes, LORD, stand firm; holiness adorns your house for endless days. (Psalm 93:1-5 NIV)

THE LORD:

1. Reigns
2. Is robed in Majesty
3. Throne established long ago
4. Is from eternity
5. Sovereign over the seas
6. Is Mighty
7. His statues stand firm
8. Holiness adorns Your house for eternity

O LORD, our Father God, You are Majestic, and Holy. You are High and Mighty and Your Word stands firm. Give us the faith to believe Your Word as the Truth and to trust You with our lives because You reign eternally. In Jesus Christ name So Be It.

Sing to the LORD, bless His name; Proclaim good tidings of His salvation from day to day. Tell of His glory, His wonderful deeds among all the peoples. For great is the LORD and He is to be feared above all gods. For all the gods of the peoples are idols, But the LORD made the heavens. Splendor and majesty are before Him, Strength and beauty are in His sanctuary. Ascribe to the LORD glory and strength. Worship the LORD; Tremble before Him, all the earth. "The LORD reigns; Indeed He will judge the peoples with equity." He is coming to judge the earth. He will judge the world in righteousness And the peoples in His faithfulness. (PSALM 96:2-13 NASB)

GOD:

1. Gives Salvation to His people
2. Is Glorious
3. Does wonderful deeds
4. Is Great and to be feared
5. Created the heavens
6. Splendor and majesty are His
7. Strong
8. Reigns
9. Will judge the peoples with fairness
10. Judge the world in Righteousness and His people in faithfulness

O Father, this is such a wonderful Psalm, help us understand the depth of truth in this praise of You. We are to worship You and tremble before You. You are Great and should be praised greatly. You will judge the world fairly and faithfully. Forgive us when we are indifferent toward You and draw us near to worship and praise You properly. Praying through the Savior's blood. So Be It

LINDA MCGREGOR CLARK

Shout joyfully to the LORD, all the earth. Serve the LORD with gladness; Come before Him with joyful singing. Know that the LORD Himself is God; It is He who has made us, and not we ourselves; We are His people and the sheep of His pasture. Enter His gates with thanksgiving And His courts with praise. Give thanks to Him, bless His name. For the LORD is good; His lovingkindness is everlasting And His faithfulness to all generations. (PSALM 100:1-5 NASB)

THE LORD:

1. Is God
2. Made us
3. We are His people
4. We are His sheep
5. Is good
6. Has everlasting love for His sheep
7. Is faithful to all generations

GOD'S PEOPLE:

1. Shout joyful praise to the LORD
2. Serve the LORD with joyful singing
3. Know God
4. Are His sheep
5. Give Him thanks and bless His name

O LORD, we are Your people, the sheep of Your pasture fill us with joy, thankfulness and praise of our God Who is good, has everlasting lovingkindness and is faithful to all His chosen! Hallelujah!

So Be It.

This pneumonia has been a tough fight! I believe I have turned a corner and have begun the last leg of this race! So I am actually singing this Psalm below! But it can be for anyone who has been struggling with a health issue or any other troubles because this is the Word of God from our God and is the absolute Truth.

Bless the LORD, O my soul, And all that is within me, bless His holy name. Bless the LORD, O my soul, And forget none of His benefits; Who pardons all your iniquities, Who heals all your diseases; Who redeems your life from the pit, Who crowns you with lovingkindness and compassion; Who satisfies your years with good things, So that your youth is renewed like the eagle. (PSALM 103:1-5 NASB)

Now this is a personal prayer of mine, but you can use it for yourself too.

O LORD, our Father, thank You for being so close to me this last week and for showing me, every day, that You have filled my life with so many benefits and you constantly forgive all Your children when we offend you, and then as we repent. Thank You, Jesus, for redeeming me from the Wrath of God with the payment of Your Blood. Thank You for surrounding me, Your child with love and compassion and thank You for the promise to renew me each day. So Be It, according to Your Word through my Redeemer and Savior, Jesus Christ.

LINDA MCGREGOR CLARK

The LORD is compassionate and gracious, Slow to anger and abounding in lovingkindness. He will not always strive with us, Nor will He keep His anger forever. He has not dealt with us according to our sins, Nor rewarded us according to our iniquities. For as high as the heavens are above the earth, So great is His lovingkindness toward those who fear Him. As far as the east is from the west, So far has He removed our transgressions from us. (Psalm 103:8-12 NASB)

SOME THINGS THE LORD IS:

1. Compassionate
2. Slow to anger
3. Abounding in lovingkindness
4. Will not always scold us
5. Will not hold His anger forever
6. Has not dealt with our sins or rewarded our wickedness
7. Has love as high as the heavens toward those who fear Him
8. Removed our sins as far as the East is from the West

Oh Father, what a wonderful reminder that You are personally involved in each of our lives. And oh how glad we are that You are patient and long suffering with Your children and You remember the Promise You made to us not to deal with us according to our wickedness! We sure need our Savior's blood to cover our sins, and we look forward to seeing You in heaven and all our fears will be gone. Show us the many times we keep sinning and give us real repentance! In Jesus Precious Name Amen

Bless the LORD, O my soul! O LORD my God, You are very great; You are clothed with splendor and majesty, Covering Yourself with light as with a cloak, He makes the clouds His chariot; He walks upon the wings of the wind; He makes the winds His messengers, Flaming fire His ministers O LORD, how many are Your works! In wisdom You have made them all. I will sing to the LORD as long as I live; I will sing praise to my God while I have my being. (PSALM 104:1-4,24,33 NASB)

O LORD, the Almighty Creator, Who is Wise and is above all, our Dear Father let us be filled with Your praises and sing to You with our whole beings! Let our thoughts and wants be pleasing to You! Fill our hearts with gladness while we are here and make us repentant children who desire to live lives pleasing to You! According to Your Word, So Be It

Oh, give thanks to the LORD, call upon His name; Make known His deeds among the peoples. Sing to Him, sing praises to Him; Speak of all His wonders. Glory in His holy name; Let the heart of those who seek the LORD be glad. Seek the LORD and His strength; Seek His face continually.
(PSALM 105:1-4 NASB)

To *glory in God's Holy name* means to take pleasure in Him, to take joy in Him, which results in other people knowing who God is by observing your lifestyle.

O Heavenly Father, the only Just and Righteous, as we go through the Psalms and see all the wonderful praise of You, we become aware of how we do not praise You like we should. So please forgive us for being unthankful for all the fantastic benefits we receive from You and teach us how to really take pleasure in You and how to please You in our praise! In Jesus Christ name Amen

Oh give thanks to the LORD, for He is good, For His lovingkindness is everlasting. Let the redeemed of the LORD say so, Whom He has redeemed from the hand of the Adversary... Let them give thanks to the LORD for His lovingkindness, And for His wonders to the sons of men! For He has satisfied the thirsty soul, And the hungry soul He has filled with what is good. (PSALM 107:1-2,8-9 NASB)

REDEEMED:

1. Tell others of their redemption from sin
2. Give thanks to the LORD for His lovingkindness

LORD:

1. Is Good
2. Lovingkindness is eternal
3. Redeemed His people from the Adversary.
4. Does Wonders to men
5. Satisfies the thirsty soul
6. Fills the hungry soul with good

O, Always Loving Father teach us to praise and worship You above all else! Give us thankful hearts that are aware of all the most wonderful grace You keep giving to us day after day and give us hungry souls to receive the good gifts from You, then fill us with Your Holy Spirit to lead us into more praise of our Good God, who is full of lovingkindness. According to Your Word, So Be It

LINDA MCGREGOR CLARK

My heart is steadfast, O God! I will sing and make melody with all my being! For your steadfast love is great above the heavens; your faithfulness reaches to the clouds. Be exalted, O God, above the heavens! Let your glory be over all the earth! (Psalm 108:1-5 ESV)

O Father, Lord of Mercy, Your love is Steadfast, but ours is not, because we have flip flopping, hot and cold hearts! Forgive us Father and fill us with Your steadfast love and faithfulness! We need Your mercy! Be exalted O God, in our hearts and give us voices full of praise to bring glory to You. In the name of Your Son, Jesus Christ, So Be It.

Praise the LORD! Blessed is the man who fears the LORD, who greatly delights in His commandments! Light dawns in the darkness for the upright; he is gracious, merciful, and righteous. It is well with the man who deals generously and lends, who conducts his affairs with justice. For the righteous will never be moved; he will be remembered forever. He is not afraid of bad news; his heart is firm, trusting in the LORD. (Psalm 112:1-7 ESV)

Person who fears the LORD:

1. joyful
2. Delights in obeying God's commands
3. Have the Light (Jesus Christ)
4. Generous
5. Compassionate
6. Righteous (obedient to God's law)
7. Lend money generously
8. Conduct business fairly
9. Never shaken by evil
10. Remembered forever
11. Not afraid of bad news
12. Heart is firm, trusting in the LORD

O Father, this list is challenging and shows us how much we need Your forgiveness and Your mercy. Give us deeper knowledge of You, so we will grow in our deep awe of You. Then the Holy Spirit can work these qualities into us to give us sound hearts that trust You LORD and are full of joyful praise! According to Your Word So Be It.

LINDA MCGREGOR CLARK

I lift up my eyes to the hills. From where does my help come? My help comes from the LORD, who made heaven and earth. He will not let your foot be moved; he who keeps you will not slumber. The LORD is your keeper; the LORD is your shade on your right hand. The sun shall not strike you by day, nor the moon by night. The LORD will keep you from all evil; he will keep your life. The LORD will keep your going out and your coming in from this time forth and forevermore. (Psalm 121:1-8 ESV)

When you see **LORD**, written in all upper-case letters, it represents God's personal name YHWH: the Self-existent One, the One Who never changes and is All Powerful.

<u>Here we have more characteristics of the LORD in relation to our faith</u>:

1. Help comes from Him, Who made Heaven and earth
2. Will not let me stumble
3. Never slumbers(naps) or sleeps
4. Watches over me; is my Keeper
5. Is my shade(protection)
6. Keeps me from all evil
7. Watches over my life to preserve my soul
8. Keeps watch over my coming and going, now and forever

O LORD, our Father God, this is a fantastic, comforting description of You, if we are Your children, the ones who are saved from Your wrath over our sin by believing Your only way to forgiveness is through Jesus. Once we are Yours, You watch over our comings and goings to preserve our souls from stumbling and to perfect the work You began in us through Jesus Christ Your Son, Hallelujah!

Out of the depths I call to you, LORD! Lord, listen to my voice; let your ears be attentive to my cry for help. LORD, if you kept an account of iniquities, LORD, who could stand? But with you there is forgiveness. I wait for the LORD; I wait and put my hope in his word. I wait for the LORD more than watchmen for the morning...put your hope in the LORD. For there is faithful love with the LORD, and with him is redemption in abundance. And he will redeem us from all our iniquities. (Psalm 130:1-8 CSB)

Heavenly Father full of mercy, there is faithful love and abundant redemption with You and You hear the prayers of Your children when we cry for help out of deep sorrow over our sins or trouble we may have. We can hope in Your forgiveness and trust in Your Word because Your Word is Truth and everlasting. Fill our hearts with hope as we wait for You. Thank You that You are continually working in us to make us ready for eternity with You to be able to give You hearty praises and thanksgivings as we grow in our knowledge of You, through Jesus Christ our Lord. Amen

LINDA MCGREGOR CLARK

Hallelujah! Praise the name of the LORD. Praise the LORD, for the LORD is good; sing praise to his name, for it is delightful. For I know that the LORD is great; our Lord is greater than all gods. The LORD does whatever he pleases in heaven and on earth, in the seas and all the depths. He causes the clouds to rise from the ends of the earth. He makes lightning for the rain and brings the wind from his storehouses. LORD, your name endures forever, your reputation, Lord, through all generations. (Psalm 135:1-13 CSB)

LORD:

1. is Good
2. Is Great
3. Does whatever He pleases in heaven and on earth, in the seas and all the depths
4. Causes the clouds to rise
5. Makes the lightening for the rain
6. Brings the wind
7. Name endures forever and His reputation through all generations

Hallelujah LORD, what a fantastic list describing our Heavenly Father the Creator of all things visible and invisible! You are the Author of all good things. You are the Good God, whose Providence rules over all, grant that we may grow to live to please You and that in all our doings we will be aware of Your fatherly mercy and assistance through Jesus Christ Your Son, So Be It.

I will bow down toward You and give thanks to Your name for Your lovingkindness and Your truth; For You have magnified Your word according to all Your name. For though the LORD is exalted, Yet He regards the lowly. Though I walk in the midst of trouble, You will revive me, Your right hand will save me. The LORD will accomplish what concerns me. (PSALM 138:2-8 NASB)

O Mighty LORD, Holy and full of Grace, Lovingkindness and Truth! We give thanks and praises to You for Your Exaulted name LORD.Thank You for caring about even us and for the promise that You will accomplish all that concerns us and will not forsake the work of Your hands! According to Your Word So Be It.

O Lord, you have searched me and known me! You know when I sit down and when I rise up; you discern my thoughts from afar. You search out my path and my lying down and are acquainted with all my ways. Even before a word is on my tongue, behold, O Lord, you know it altogether. You hem me in, behind and before, and lay your hand upon me. Such knowledge is too wonderful for me; it is high; I cannot attain it. (Psalm 139:1-6 ESV)

The LORD, God our Father:

1. Examines our heart
2. Knows everything about us
3. Knows when we sit or stand
4. Knows our thoughts even when we are far off
5. Sees us when we travel or rest at home
6. Knows everything we do
7. Knows what we are going to say, even before we say it
8. Encircles us
9. Places His hand on us

O God our Father, this is such wonderful knowledge for us, it is hard to comprehend how much You love Your children and how deeply You know us, care for us and protect us, even when we are completely unaware. This knowledge also makes us aware of our need to constantly be repenting, because of our evil thoughts, wicked hearts and our tongue that says bad words or tells lies. O thank You Jesus, for paying our debt of sin and thank You Holy Spirit for working in our lives to help us understand all this Truth and to make us more like Jesus, in Whose Name we say this prayer, Amen

Where shall I go from your Spirit? Or where shall I flee from your presence? If I ascend to heaven, you are there! If I make my bed in Sheol, you are there! If I take the wings of the morning and dwell in the uttermost parts of the sea, even there your hand shall lead me, and your right hand shall hold me. If I say, "Surely the darkness shall cover me, and the light about me be night," even the darkness is not dark to you; the night is bright as the day, for darkness is as light with you. (Psalm 139:7-12 ESV)

THOUGHTS:

This has always been a special group of verses to me, which I have memorized. Because it assures me that there is no where I can go or anyone can take me that my God is not there! And it also reminds me that God watching me every moment, so I need to be aware of how I am behaving, am I doing anything that I would not do if Jesus was standing next to me or is there something I should be doing.

O Father, what a wonderful, fantastic promise to Your children!! There is absolutely no place we can go, or someone can take us, where You are not there with Your right hand of Power holding us and leading us. Even darkness is as light to You! Thank You, thank You Heavenly Father!
Holy Spirit fill us with confidence that we can trust You in any situation, no matter how frustrating, scary, or painful. According to Your Word, O Father, So Be It.

LINDA MCGREGOR CLARK

For you formed my inward parts; you knitted me together in my mother's womb. I praise you, for I am fearfully and wonderfully made. Wonderful are your works; my soul knows it very well. My frame was not hidden from you, when I was being made in secret, intricately woven in the depths of the earth. Your eyes saw my unformed substance; in your book were written, every one of them, the days that were formed for me, when as yet there was none of them. How precious to me are your thoughts, O God! How vast is the sum of them! If I would count them, they are more than the sand. I awake, and I am still with you. (Psalm 139:13-18 ESV)

THOUGHTS:

These verses are important in the fight against abortion. If you believe these words of God then He is designing each part of each baby in the Mother's womb and to kill the baby is totally against the law of God, where He says "You shall not murder." These verses also tell us to be content and to praise God for how He made us.

O Father, how deep are the riches of Your wisdom and knowledge, how beyond our understanding are Your judgements and Your ways. Yet You take time to give us these words to show us how important we are to You and how involved You are with each baby, even before birth. What wonderful thoughts to contemplate that You knew us before we existed and then knit us together in our Mother's womb! Forgive us for not being thankful and for just living as if You do not exist! Draw us closer to You through Jesus and fill us with wonder and thankfulness at Your creation. According to Your Word So Be It.

Search me, O God, and know my heart! Try me and know my thoughts! And see if there be any grievous way in me and lead me in the way everlasting! (Psalm 139:23-24 ESV)

THOUGHTS:

Here is a example of some verses that are a perfect prayer to repeat back to our Heavenly Father exactly as written or by personalizing like the folowing prayer:

O God, You know everything about me, what is in my heart and all my thoughts. You even know me better then I know myself. Show me the things in me that offend You, give me a repentant heart and lead me in the narrow way that leads to eternity with You. Because of Your Son, our Savior and Lord, Jesus Christ, So Be It.

LORD, I call on you; hurry to help me. Listen to my voice when I call on you. May my prayer be set before you as incense, the raising of my hands as the evening offering. LORD, set up a guard for my mouth; keep watch at the door of my lips. Do not let my heart turn to any evil thing or perform wicked acts. (Psalm 141:1-5 CSB)

LORD, we call on You, please help us, please listen to our voices and may our prayer be pleasing to You. Set a guard over our mouths and keep watch at the door of our lips. Keep our hearts from evil and from following wicked men, who entice us with things that look delightful. When a good person corrects us firmly, help us understand it is because they love us. Then make us willing to listen and obey. We ask that You give us perfect assurance and confidence in answered prayer because of Jesus's obedience and sacrifice, then may we be counted among those who are redeemed by His blood. So Be It.

Let me hear of your unfailing love each morning, for I am trusting you. Show me where to walk, for I give myself to you... Teach me to do your will, for you are my God. May your gracious Spirit lead me forward on a firm footing. For the glory of your name, O Lord, preserve my life. Because of your faithfulness, bring me out of this distress. (Psalm 143:8 & 10-11 NLT)

THOUGHTS:

This is a prayer from King David, who is desiring that God in His steadfast love will show him how to live according to God's will. He is asking for the Holy Spirit to lead him to be faithful.

Dear Father, we need to hear of Your unfailing love every day through Your Psalms! Continue to guide us and fill our hearts with pure trust of You. O Holy Spirit lead us forward on firm footing to bring glory to Your faithfulness as You bring us out of distressing times. We need You!! In Jesus Christ name may it be so!

LINDA MCGREGOR CLARK

I will exalt you, my God and King, and praise your name forever and ever. I will praise you every day; yes. Great is the LORD! He is most worthy of praise! No one can measure his greatness. Let each generation tell its children of your mighty acts. I will meditate on your majestic, glorious splendor and your wonderful miracles. I will proclaim your greatness. (Psalm 145:1-7 NLT)

O HOLY SPIRIT help us to know the LORD God our King so well, that we are like this Psalm, full of praises about His Greatness, which no one can measure. Make us aware of our responsibilities to tell our family, so they will know how wonderful our Father God is and the Great things He has done. Forgive us, Father, for not giving You the credit for the wonderful goodness from You in our lives. Forgive us for not being children who are excited that we have a Father, Who is Majestic, full of Glorious Splendor and Who does awe inspiring deeds for His children. We need to know You better, Please Father, so we can really praise You with much thanksgiving, all the days of our lives, through Jesus Christ Your Son, So Be It.

The LORD is merciful and compassionate, slow to get angry and filled with unfailing love. The LORD is good to everyone. He showers compassion on all his creation. All of your works will thank you, LORD, and your faithful followers will praise you. They will speak of the glory of your kingdom; they will give examples of your power. They will tell about your mighty deeds and about the majesty and glory of your reign. For your kingdom is an everlasting kingdom. You rule throughout all generations. The LORD always keeps his promises; he is gracious in all he does. (Psalm 145:8-13 NLT)

LORD:

1. Gracious and Merciful
2. Slow to anger
3. Abounding in steadfast love
4. Good to all
5. Merciful over all His creation
6. Receiving thanks from all His works
7. Blessed by all His Saints (faithful followers)
8. Has a Glorious Kingdom, that is everlasting
9. Dominion endures forever
10. Faithful in all His Words
11. Kind in all His works

O my LORD, what an awesome list of some of Your character traits. Give us understanding of these and fill our hearts with praise and joy, as we read Your words in the Bible.

Forgive us for being grumbling and complaining children, instead of praising You in all situations. Thank You for being Slow to anger, because we are disobedient children and do not live our lives to please You, but to please ourselves. Help us LORD. We pray asking these things, because of Your Son, Jesus. So Be It.

LINDA MCGREGOR CLARK

For your kingdom is an everlasting kingdom. You rule throughout all generations. The LORD always keeps his promises; he is gracious in all he does. The LORD helps the fallen and lifts those bent beneath their loads. The eyes of all look to you in hope; you give them their food as they need it. When you open your hand, you satisfy the hunger and thirst of every living thing. The LORD is righteous in everything he does; he is filled with kindness. The LORD is close to all who call on him, yes, to all who call on him in truth. He grants the desires of those who fear him; he hears their cries for help and rescues them. The LORD protects all those who love him, but he destroys the wicked. I will praise the LORD and may everyone on earth bless his holy name forever and ever. (Psalm 145:13-21 NLT)

LORD:

1. Has an everlasting kingdom
2. Rules throughout all generations
3. Always keeps His promises
4. Is gracious in all He does
5. Helps those who fall
6. Raises all who are bowed down
7. Gives food to all who look to Him
8. Satisfies the desire of every living thing
9. Righteous in all His ways
10. Kind in all His works
11. Near to all who call on Him in Truth
12. Fulfills the desire of those who fear Him, hears their cry, and saves them
13. Preserves all who love Him
14. Destroys all the wicked

O LORD, we will praise You always, Your praise will continually be in our mouths! What an awesome God we have as Father!

One Who helps us when we stumble or when our spirit is full of sadness. A God Who is near when we call out for help and Who hears our prayers. Holy Spirit fill us with true fear of the LORD, with understanding of His Truth and trust of His ways. According to His Word, So Be It.

LINDA MCGREGOR CLARK

Praise the LORD! Let all that I am praise the LORD. I will praise the LORD as long as I live. I will sing praises to my God with my dying breath. Do not put your confidence in other people; there is no help for you there. When they breathe their last, they return to the earth, and all their plans die with them. But joyful are those who have God as their helper, whose hope is in the LORD their God. He made heaven and earth, the sea, and everything in them. He keeps every promise forever. The LORD opens the eyes of the blind. The LORD lifts up those who are weighed down. The LORD loves the godly. The LORD protects us. He cares for the orphans and widows, but he frustrates the plans of the wicked. The LORD will reign forever. He will be your God throughout the generations. Praise the LORD! (Psalm 146:1-10 NLT)

What should I do?

1. Praise the LORD with all I am as long as I live
2. Praise the LORD with my dying breath
3. Do not put my confidence in other people
4. Be joyful in God, as my Helper

LORD:

1. Made heaven and earth, the seas and everything
2. Keeps every promise forever
3. Gives understanding
4. Lifts those who are weighed down
5. Loves the godly and protects us
6. Cares for orphans and widows
7. Reigns forever

O LORD, our Heavenly Father, we need Your help to really praise You in the way You deserve to be praised. Help us to genuinely believe that You keep every promise You have made in Your Word and that we can depend on You to care for us. We need You to open our eyes to Truth and to faith that You will be our God forever. Through the blood of Jesus, So Be It

PSALM 119

❖

Matthew Henry – the great 18th-century Bible commentator – was introduced to Psalm 119 as a child. His father, Philip Henry, told his children to take one verse of Psalm 119 every morning to meditate on, and thereby go through the entire Psalm twice in the year. Philip said to his children, "That will bring you to be in love with all the rest of the Scriptures." Perhaps that practice was why Matthew Henry loved the Bible so much that he wrote a commentary that is used still today.

We won't go exactly verse by verse, but we will go section by section. Each section is 8 verses and there are 22 sections, each section representing a letter of the Hebrew alphabet and each line in a section begins with that letter. It is an acrostic pattern. Can you imagine writing 176 verses divided into 22 sections and each 8 verses must begin with the same letter! But God....

Heavenly Father, I ask You to fill us with the desire to seek You with all our hearts and to diligently keep Your way, as we pray through Psalm 119. I pray that we will learn to love Your word with all our hearts and to store Your word in our hearts, so we won't sin against You. Open our eyes to see wonderful things in Your word. According to Your Word So Be It.

You have ordained Your precepts, that we should keep them diligently. Oh that my ways may be established To keep Your statutes! Then I shall not be ashamed When I look upon all Your commandments. I shall give thanks to You with uprightness of heart, When I learn Your righteous judgments. I shall keep Your statutes; Do not forsake me utterly! (Psalms 119:4-8 NASB)

THOUGHTS:

Psalm 119 is all about the glory of the Word of God and the author uses at least 8 different words to describe the scriptures. In these five verses, he uses precepts, statues (twice), commandments, and righteous judgments to refer to the scriptures.

We see that:

1. God ordained His precepts to be kept diligently
2. We are to keep God's statues diligently
3. We will praise God correctly, when we learn His righteous judgments

O Holy Spirit, You are our Teacher and we ask that You give us understanding as we begin our time in Psalm 119. Help us be diligent to keep God's commandments and fill us with a love for the scriptures and make us correct praisers of God. Praying in Jesus Christ Name, So Be It.

LINDA MCGREGOR CLARK

How can a young man keep his way pure? By guarding it according to your word. With my whole heart I seek you; let me not wander from your commandments! I have stored up your word in my heart, that I might not sin against you. Blessed are you, O Lord; teach me your statutes! I will meditate on your precepts and fix my eyes on your ways. I will delight in your statutes; I will not forget your word. (Psalm 119:9-12, 15-16 ESV)

This was written to the author's son, but these verses can be applied to anyone.

God's Word:

1. word(3 times)
2. Commandments
3. statues(twice)
4. Precepts

The wonderful thing about these verses is they make a great prayer:

Dearest Father God, the Author of the Bible, Help us to keep our ways pure as we guard them according to Your Word. Give us hearts that diligently seek You and keep us from wondering from Your commandments. Help us to store Your Word in our hearts to keep us from sinning against You. O LORD teach us Your statues, help us to remember Your precepts and to focus on Your ways, so we won't forget Your word, which will keep us pure. According to Your will, So Be It.

Deal bountifully with your servant, that I may live and keep your word. Open my eyes, that I may behold wondrous things out of your law. My soul is consumed with longing for your rules at all times. Your testimonies are my delight; they are my counselors. (Psalm 119:17- 24 ESV)

GOD'S WORD:

1. Word
2. Law
3. Rules
4. testimonies
5. counselors

There is the word "Delight" again. My deep desire through this study of Psalm 119 is that we gain a delight (pleasure, enjoyment) and love of God's Word.

Most Merciful God the Author of all good, Who has given Your holy commandments to us, engrave them in our hearts. Let us see our sins and repent, that our whole delight will be in Your law and we will be governed by Your Holy Word to gain that eternal salvation which You promised, through Christ Jesus, Your Son. Amen (From The Scottish Psalter, 1595, p.125)

LINDA MCGREGOR CLARK

When I told of my plans, you answered me; teach me your statutes! Make me understand the way of your precepts, and I will meditate on your wondrous works. Put false ways far from me and graciously teach me your law! I have chosen the way of faithfulness; I set your rules before me. I cling to your testimonies, O Lord; let me not be put to shame! I will run in the way of your commandments for you enlarge my heart! (Psalm 119:26-32 ESV)

"Enter through the narrow gate; for the gate is wide and the way is broad that leads to destruction, and there are many who enter through it. For the gate is small and the way is narrow that leads to life, and there are few who find it. (Matthew 7:13-14 NASB)

THOUGHTS:

We just read that the Psalmist has asked God for understanding of the (narrow) way of His precepts and he has chosen the (narrow) way of faithfulness and commits to run in the (narrow) way of God's commandments. All because God will enlarge his heart.

Verses 31-32 are extra special for us to store in our hearts: I have chosen the way of faithfulness, I set Your rules before me, I cling to Your testimonies, O Lord...I will run in the way of Your commandments for You enlarge my heart!

O Father fill us with these same desires to understand Your narrow way, so we will be Your faithful children. Teach us that Your laws are the narrow way and keep us from the broad way that leads to destruction.Praying in Jesus Christ name So Be It.

Teach me your decrees, O Lord; I will keep them to the end. Give me understanding and I will obey your instructions; I will put them into practice with all my heart. Make me walk along the path of your commands, for that is where my happiness is found. Give me an eagerness for your laws rather than a love for money! Turn my eyes from worthless things and give me life through your word. (Psalms 119:33-37 NLT)

GOD'S WORD:

1. Decrees
2. Instructions
3. Commands
4. Laws
5. word.

Again, this section of verses can be used as a prayer that will be according to God's will.

O Lord teach us Your decrees and give us hearts that will keep them always. Give us understanding of Your instructions, so we will obey them. Make us walk in the narrow path of Your commands for that's where our happiness is found. Cause us to love Your laws rather than money. According to Your laws So Be It.

LINDA MCGREGOR CLARK

Let your steadfast love come to me, O Lord, your salvation according to your promise; then shall I have an answer for him who taunts me, for I trust in your word. I will keep your law continually, forever and ever, for I find my delight in your commandments, which I love. I will lift up my hands toward your commandments, which I love, and I will meditate on your statutes. (Psalm 119:41-48 ESV)

According to the Bible, how do God's children behave:

1. Trust in His word
2. Obey His law forever
3. Love and delight in His commands
4. Meditate on His statues

O Dear Lord let Your steadfast love come to us, Your salvation that You promised. Help us to trust in Your word and to keep Your law forever. Fill us with love for Your commands. Asking in Your Son's name Amen

Remember your promise to me; it is my only hope. Your promise revives me; it comforts me in all my troubles. I meditate on your age-old regulations; O Lord, they comfort me. I become furious with the wicked, because they reject your instructions. Your decrees have been the theme of my songs wherever I have lived. I reflect at night on who you are, O Lord; therefore, I obey your instructions. This is how I spend my life: obeying your commandments. (Psalms 119:49-56 NLT)

God's Word:

1. Promise comforts in all my troubles
2. My only Hope
3. age-old regulations
4. Instructions are rejected by the wicked
5. Decrees are the theme of my songs
6. commandments.

Such descriptive words explaining what the Bible really is and why it's so important!

O Father open our eyes to understand the preciousness of Your word given to Your children.
O Holy Spirit show us how the Bible gives us hope and comfort in trouble, gives us joy and songs to sing, how it helps us grow in our knowledge of God and helps us to obey God's rules.
In the name of God's Son, Jesus Christ, So Be It.

The Lord is my portion; I have promised to keep your words. I have sought your favor with all my heart; be gracious to me according to your promise. I thought about my ways and turned my steps back to your decrees. I hurried, not hesitating to keep your commands. Though the ropes of the wicked were wrapped around me, I did not forget your instruction. I rise at midnight to thank you for your righteous judgments. I am a friend to all who fear you, to those who keep your precepts. Lord, the earth is filled with your faithful love; teach me your statutes. (Psalm 119:57-64 CSB)

GOD'S WORD:

1. Words
2. Promise
3. Decrees
4. Commands
5. Instruction
6. Judgments
7. Precepts
8. Statues

O Father God help us to be like the Psalmist, who examined his ways and returned to obedience of Your decrees. Teach us that You are faithful to Your words and love Your children. Trusting Your promises Amen

Teach me good judgment and knowledge, for I believe in your commandments. You are good and do good; teach me your statutes...with my whole heart I keep your precepts; I delight in your law.
(Psalm 119:66-70 ESV)

GOD'S WORD:

1. Commandments
2. Statues
3. Precepts
4. Law

O Father God, You are good and do good, teach us good judgment and knowledge as we believe in Your commandments. Give us hearts that delight in Your law and keep Your precepts. In Jesus Christ name So Be It.

LINDA MCGREGOR CLARK

Your hands have made and fashioned me; give me understanding that I may learn your commandments. Those who fear you shall see me and rejoice, because I have hoped in your word. I know, O Lord, that your rules are righteous, and that in faithfulness you have afflicted me. Let your steadfast love comfort me according to your promise to your servant. Let your mercy come to me, that I may live; for your law is my delight. I will meditate on your precepts. Let those who fear you turn to me, they that know your testimonies. Let my heart be sound in your statutes, that I may not be put to shame! (Psalms 119:73-80 ESV)

THOUGHTS:

After we lost, our son, Darrell, I came upon this section and fell in love with these verses. Each verse has special meaning for me in my sorrow. I hope you will go slowly through these words from God and let the Holy Spirit give you understanding and encouragement for whatever place in which you are at this time, whether you have lost someone or are suffering from illness.

O Father, we need sound hearts in Your Word, so we can hope in Your promises no matter what happens in our lives or in our families. We need Your mercy and comfort. Asking in Jesus's name Amen

My soul longs for your salvation; I hope in your word. My eyes long for your promise; I ask, "When will you comfort me?" For...I have not forgotten your statutes. All your commandments are sure; help me...I have not forsaken your precepts. In your steadfast love give me life, that I may keep the testimonies of your mouth. (Psalm 119:81-88 ESV)

THOUGHTS:

This section of Psalm 119 is from a deeply sad child of God, who is begging his Father for help, yet he's clinging onto God's word, which is called His promise, statues, commandments, precepts and testimonies.

The actions of God's child are:

1. longing for salvation (for help)
2. Hoping in the Word
3. Asking for comfort
4. Trusting in God's commandments
5. Not forsaking God's precepts
6. Keeping God's testimonies

Oh Father, it's so hard when things are not how we want. But we can be sure that You are always here to give us hope in Your word. Thank You for the comfort which comes from Your steadfast love revealed in Your statues. According to Your testimonies So Be It.

LINDA MCGREGOR CLARK

Forever, O Lord, your word is firmly fixed in the heavens. Your faithfulness endures to all generations; you have established the earth, and it stands fast. By your appointment they stand this day, for all things are your servants. If your law had not been my delight, I would have perished in my affliction. I will never forget your precepts, for by them you have given me life. I am yours; save me, for I have sought your precepts. I have seen a limit to all perfection, but your commandment is exceedingly broad. (Psalm 119:89-96 ESV)

GOD's WORD:

1. Forever
2. Firmly fixed in heaven
3. Law
4. Precepts
5. Commandments are without limit

GOD:

1. Faithful thru all generations
2. Made the earth
3. All things are His servants

Dear Faithful Father God give us understanding to learn precepts, so we will delight in Your Word. In Jesus Christ name So Be It.

Oh, how I love your law! It is my meditation all the day. Your commandment makes me wiser than my enemies, for it is ever with me…I hold back my feet from every evil way, in order to keep your word. I do not turn aside from your rules, for you have taught me. How sweet are your words to my taste, sweeter than honey to my mouth! Through your precepts I get understanding; therefore, I hate every false way. (Psalm 119:97-104ESV)

GOD'S WORD:

1. Law
2. Commandment
3. Word
4. Rules
5. Precepts

O Father fill our hearts with love for Your law, so we will have wisdom and will turn away from every evil way. Give us understanding as we read Your precepts, so we will hate every false way. According to Your Word So Be It.

Your word is a lamp for my feet, a light on my path. I have taken an oath and confirmed it, that I will follow your righteous laws. Accept, Lord, the willing praise of my mouth, and teach me your laws. Your statutes are my heritage forever; they are the joy of my heart. My heart is set on keeping your decrees to the very end. (Psalm 119:105-112 NIV)

GOD'S WORD;

1. Word
2. Lamp and light for our path
3. Righteous laws
4. Statues
5. Decrees

Heavenly Father, Your word is our guide through this world, teach us Your laws and make them the joy of our hearts. Set our hearts on keeping Your decrees to the very end. In Jesus Christ name Amen

$\mathbf{Y}$ou are my refuge and my shield; your word is my source of hope. Lord, sustain me as you promised, that I may live! Do not let my hope be crushed. Sustain me, and I will be rescued; then I will meditate continually on your decrees. (Psalm 119:114-117 NLT)

GOD's WORD:

1. Word is Source of hope
2. Promise
3. Decrees (directions, laws)

O God, You are our hiding place and our shield from evil. Through Your word we get hope, so fill our hearts with the desire to know Your decrees fully. In Your Son's name we ask Amen

My eyes fail with longing for Your salvation and for Your righteous word. Deal with Your servant according to Your lovingkindness and teach me Your statutes. I am Your servant; give me understanding, that I may know Your testimonies. It is time for the LORD to act, for they have broken Your law. I love Your commandments above gold, yes, above fine gold. Therefore, I esteem right all Your precepts concerning everything, I hate every false way. (Psalm 119:123-128 NASB)

GOD'S WORD:

1. Righteous Word
2. Statues
3. Testimonies
4. Law
5. Commandments
6. Precepts

O Father in Your lovingkindness teach us Your statues and give us understanding so we will know Your testimonies. Fill our hearts with love of Your precepts and hate of every false way. According to Your will So Be It.

Υour testimonies are wonderful; therefore, my soul keeps them. The unfolding of your words gives light; it imparts understanding to the simple. I open my mouth and pant, because I long for your commandments. Turn to me and be gracious to me, as is your way with those who love your name. Keep steady my steps according to your promise, and let no iniquity get dominion over me. Make your face shine upon your servant, and teach me your statutes. My eyes shed streams of tears, because people do not keep your law. (Psalm 119:129-136 ESV)

GOD's WORD:

1. Testimonies
2. Words
3. Commandments
4. Promise
5. Statues
6. Law

GOD's CHILD:

1. Keeps God's testimonies
2. Longs for God's commandments
3. Loves God's name
4. Prays for steady steps and that no sin will dominate
5. Cries because people don't keep God's law

Dear Holy Spirit our Teacher and Counselor, this list of characteristics of a child of God makes me sad because we don't live fully like this. We break God's laws every day and we're not sad. Please make us aware of our sins and give us repentant hearts. Fill us with love for God and a longing to obey. In Jesus Christ name So Be It.

LINDA MCGREGOR CLARK

O Lord, you are righteous, and your regulations are fair. Your laws are perfect and completely trustworthy. Your promises have been thoroughly tested; that is why I love them so much. Your justice is eternal, and your instructions are perfectly true. As pressure and stress bear down on me, I find joy in your commands. Your laws are always right; help me to understand them so I may live. (Psalm 119:137-144 NLT)

GOD's WORD:

1. Regulations
2. Laws
3. Promises
4. Instructions
5. Commands

O Lord Your regulations are totally perfect and completely trustworthy. Everything about Your laws is always right. Give us understanding, so we will obey Your commands and when we don't obey, make us aware of our disobedience and cause us to repent. Through the Blood of Jesus's sacrifice So Be It.

I cried with all my heart; answer me, O LORD! I will observe Your statutes. I cried to You; save me And I shall keep Your testimonies. I rise before dawn and cry for help; I wait for Your words. My eyes anticipate the night watches, That I may meditate on Your word. Hear my voice according to Your lovingkindness; Revive me, O LORD, according to Your ordinances. You are near, O LORD, And all Your commandments are truth. Of old I have known from Your testimonies That You have founded them forever. (Psalm 119:145-152 NASB)

THOUGHTS:

Remember when LORD is in all uppercase letters it is referring to God's personal name YHWH (I AM), The One Who Is The Self-Existent One.

In this section of Psalm 119, the Psalmist is very sad and crying out to the LORD for help. Yet even in his pain he knows the LORD is near and His Word can be trusted.

GOD'S WORD:

1. Statues
2. Testimonies
3. Words
4. Ordinances
5. Commandments

LORD our Father this is a special picture of one of Your children going through a sad and emotional time. Teach us how to trust You when things are painful or scary or not what we want. Because of Your love for Your children Amen

The sum of your word is truth, and every one of your righteous rules endures forever. (Psalm 119:160 ESV)

O Father this is a wonderful summary of Your Word the Bible. It is totally True and Righteous and endures forever! Thank You, thank You for giving us Your Word in language we understand, so we can know You better and know what You expect from us. Open our eyes to understand and make our hearts obedient. In Jesus Christ name Amen

I rejoice at your word like one who finds great treasure. Seven times a day I praise you for your righteous rules. Great peace have those who love your law; nothing can make them stumble. I hope for your salvation, O Lord, and I do your commandments. My soul keeps your testimonies; I love them exceedingly. I keep your precepts and testimonies, for all my ways are before you. (Psalm 119:162-168 ESV)

GOD's WORD:

1. Great treasure
2. Righteous rules
3. Law
4. Commandments
5. Testimonies
6. Precepts

GOD's CHILDREN's LIFESTYLE:

1. Rejoice at the Treasure
2. Praise God all day for rules
3. Love the law and have peace and no stumbling
4. Have hope
5. Are obedient
6. Live knowing all their ways are before God

Dear Father, make us rejoicing, praising, obedient children, who love Your Bible. Asking according to Your Word, So Be It.

LINDA MCGREGOR CLARK

Let my cry come before you, O Lord; give me understanding according to your word! My lips will pour forth praise, for you teach me your statutes. My tongue will sing of your word, for all your commandments are right. (Psalm 119:169-172 ESV)

Our God this time we've spent in Psalm 119 has been very special as we have read all about how precious Your Bible is for us to read and study diligently. As we go about our lives please bring back to our minds some of the verses to encourage us to live according to Your commands. According to Your promises, So Be It.

How happy is the one who does not walk in the advice of the wicked or stand in the pathway with sinners or sit in the company of mockers! Instead, his delight is in the Lord's instruction, and he meditates on it day and night. He is like a tree planted beside flowing streams that bears its fruit in its season and whose leaf does not wither. Whatever he does prospers. The wicked are not like this; instead, they are like chaff that the wind blows away. Therefore, the wicked will not stand up in the judgment, nor sinners in the assembly of the righteous. For the Lord watches over the way of the righteous, but the way of the wicked leads to ruin. (Psalm 1:1-6 CSB)

CHAFF: worthless shells off the seeds that are thrown away and burned.

THOUGHTS:

Psalm 1 explains why we've spent all this time in Psalm 119. The more times we delight in God's Word, the more blessed we are in our life of faith.

O Merciful and Heavenly Father who has created us for blessedness and joy and have given us Your holy law which is our only rule and measure showing us how we should live well and godly. By Your grace make us renounce our own sins and desires, also, all evil company. Then may we bring forth the fruits of the Spirit and always be under Your holy protection. So, when Your Son Jesus Christ shall appear, we may be counted among those who are redeemed by His Blood. So Be It. (Prayer from Scottish Psalter of 1595)

LINDA MCGREGOR CLARK

EPHESIANS

❖

Beginning today we are going to go through the letter written by Paul to the churches around Ephesus. Paul wanted them to know God's eternal plans for all humanity, Jews and Gentiles alike. The first 3 chapters are about what Christians believe and God's grace through Jesus Christ, then the last 3 chapters explain how God's grace works in our lives and shows us how we should live. Paul probably wrote this letter while he was in prison in Rome about A. D. 60.

This letter is from Paul, chosen by the will of God to be an apostle of Christ Jesus. I am writing to God's holy people in Ephesus, who are faithful followers of Christ Jesus. May God our Father and the Lord Jesus Christ give you grace and peace. (Ephesians 1:1-2 NLT)

O our Father God, we thank You for the faithfulness of Paul to write these words of Yours and for our opportunity to read them and know You better. Also, help us to understand better how we are blessed and loved by You through Jesus's sacrifice and how we are to live our lives in this world to bring glory to You. May You God our Father and the Lord Jesus Christ give us grace and peace. Amen

All praise to God, the Father of our Lord Jesus Christ, who has blessed us with every spiritual blessing in the heavenly realms because we are united with Christ. Even before he made the world, God loved us and chose us in Christ to be holy and without fault in his eyes. (Ephesians 1:3-4 NLT)

GOD:

1. All praise to Him
2. Father of Jesus
3. Blessed us with every spiritual blessing in heaven
4. Created the world
5. Before creation He loved and chose us to be holy in Jesus

WOW Father, Your Word says You chose Your children before You created the world and even loved us first! Also, through being united with Jesus, we are totally blessed with every spiritual blessing! O Father help us to show this truth through our daily lives and thank You, thank You, thank You for forgiveness and for Jesus's blood sacrifice that made this blessed Truth possible. In Jesus Christ name So Be It.

God decided in advance to adopt us into his own family by bringing us to himself through Jesus Christ. This is what he wanted to do, and it gave him great pleasure. So, we praise God for the glorious grace he has poured out on us who belong to his dear Son. (Ephesians 1:5-6 NLT)

GOD:

1. Predestined us for adoption
2. Brought us to Himself through Jesus
3. Blesses us with grace
4. Is due our praises

Dear Father, we're so glad and thankful You loved us so much that You chose us to be Your children and You are always working in our lives through Your grace, lavishing it on those of us who belong to Jesus. Help us live daily lives of praise and thankfulness to You for choosing us to be Your children. In Jesus Christ name Amen

In Jesus we have redemption through His blood, the forgiveness of our trespasses, according to the riches of God's grace which He lavished on us. (Ephesians 1:7-8 NASB)

O Father, this description of Your grace as so abundant and rich and as lavished on us through Jesus is a wonderful picture of the full and free forgiveness we have received because of the shed blood of Jesus, our Savior! Hallelujah What a Savior! Hallelujah What a Loving Gracious Father! We are so undeserving of Your forgiveness, but so thankful for it!! According to Your Word So Be It.

God has now revealed to us his mysterious will regarding Christ—which is to fulfill his own good plan. And this is God's plan: At the right time he will bring everything together under the authority of Christ—everything in heaven and on earth. (Ephesians 1:9-10 NLT)

O our Father Sovereign Commander of the universe, thank You for telling Your children in the Bible all about Your plan for this world in which we live. Thank You that we can look forward to the time when Christ Jesus will show His authority and everyone on earth will bow before Him either in fear or in worship and praise! In Jesus Powerful Name So Be It

LINDA MCGREGOR CLARK

In Christ we have also received an inheritance, because we were predestined according to the plan of God who works out everything in agreement with the purpose of his will, (Ephesians 1:11 CSB)

O Father, what a wonderful thing to know that as Your children we have been part of Your plan for this world from before creation and we have an inheritance waiting for us in heaven! Thank You for always working everything according to Your perfect grace filled will. Help us to live each day in this confidence that You are always in control and working all things for Your glory and our good. In Jesus Christ name So Be It.

In Christ you, also, when you heard the word of truth, the gospel of your salvation, and believed in Him, were sealed with the promised Holy Spirit, who is the guarantee of our inheritance until we acquire possession of it, to the praise of His glory. (Ephesians 1:13-14 ESV)

HOLY SPIRIT:

1. Seals those God saves into Jesus
2. Is the Promised One
3. Is the guarantee of our inheritance
4. Brings praise to God

O God the Holy Spirit, teach us the truth we are reading from the Bible and help us learn daily that in ourselves we are sinful but through Jesus' sacrifice, and Your sealing us into the Family, we will get to heaven, because our sin is forgiven! Fill our lives with praising of God, so others will see and be drawn to You. Thank You Father for choosing us! Thank You Jesus for our salvation! Thank You Holy Spirit for sealing us in the Family and being our Teacher! In Jesus Christ name So Be It.

LINDA MCGREGOR CLARK

I do not cease to give thanks for you, remembering you in my prayers, that the God of our Lord Jesus Christ, the Father of glory, may give you the Spirit of wisdom and of understanding in the knowledge of God, having the eyes of your hearts enlightened, so you may know the hope to which God has called you, the riches of his glorious inheritance in the saints, and the immeasurable greatness of his power toward us who believe, according to the working of his great might. (Ephesians 1:16-19 ESV)

GOD:

1. Father of glory
2. Gives us the Spirit for wisdom and understanding in order to know Him
3. Enlightens our hearts
4. Call us to hope in our inheritance
5. Has Great power that cannot be measured

O Father of glory and immeasurable power, we need Your wisdom and need understanding, so please fill our hearts with hope and strong belief in Your plan for our lives and for our coming inheritance because of Jesus's sacrifice! We believe, help us in our unbelief. In Jesus Christ name Amen

God's mighty power raised Christ from the dead and seated him in the place of honor at God's right hand in the heavenly realms. Now he is far above any ruler or authority or power or leader or anything else—not only in this world but also in the world to come. God has put all things under the authority of Christ and has made him head over all things for the benefit of the church. And the church is Christ's body; it is made full and complete by Christ, who fills all things everywhere with himself. (Ephesians 1:20-23 NLT)

JESUS CHRIST:

1. God's mighty power raised Him from the dead
2. Is seated at God's right hand in heaven
3. Is above all rule, authority, power, and dominion
4. Is above every name, now and forever
5. All things are under His feet
6. Is the Head of the church
7. Church is His body
8. Fills all in all

O Father, what a wonderful, powerful, majestic description of Jesus and to think He, Who is over everything, is our Savior! Holy Spirit, please keep this Truth locked in our minds and hearts as we go through this day and give us much comfort as we have confidence in Jesus's authority and power to work everything for Your glory and our good. In the Powerful Name of Jesus Christ Amen

And you were dead in your trespasses and sins in which you previously lived according to the ways of this world, according to the ruler of the power of the air, the spirit now working in the disobedient. We too all previously lived among them in our fleshly desires, carrying out the inclinations of our flesh and thoughts, and we were by nature children under wrath as the others were also. **But God,** who is rich in mercy, because of his great love that he had for us, made us alive with Christ even though we were dead in trespasses. You are saved by grace! (Ephesians 2:1-5 CSB)

THOUGHTS:

Those two words "But God" are a wonderful introduction to God doing something to counteract evil. Be sure to notice when you see "But God" come into a passage you are reading. In these verses God is pulling us out of the old life of sin and making us alive in Him to be saved by grace. What a Great God we have!

O Father, thank You, thank You, thank You for the words "BUT GOD"!! we were definitely dead in sin and not the least interested in holiness or obeying You, But You greatly loved us and are full of mercy, so you made us alive through Jesus simply by Your grace! We are so underserving and yet so blessed! In Jesus Christ name Amen

For by grace you have been saved through faith. And this is not your own doing; it is the gift of God, not a result of your own works, so that none of us may boast. For we are his workmanship, created in Christ Jesus for good works, which God prepared beforehand, that we should do them. (Ephesians 2:8-10 ESV)

THOUGHTS:

Oh I am so glad that God does all the work to get us into the family of God, because I am sure I would still be in the darkness without any hope. But once God saves us He reveals the life of good works that He has created for each of us to do.

O Father, what a fantastic gift we have received of being saved from Your wrath over our sins by Your choosing us and giving us the gift of grace and faith!! Thank You that this gift is not something we have to earn or can earn but it is a Gift because of Jesus's sacrifice. O Holy Spirit help us to do the good works that God has called us to do, now that we are in His Family. In Jesus Christ name Amen

LINDA MCGREGOR CLARK

But do not take any of this for granted(being saved by grace). It was only yesterday that you were outsiders to God's ways, had no idea of any of this, did not know the first thing about the way God works, and had not the faintest idea of Christ. You knew nothing of that rich history of God's covenants and promises to Israel and had not a clue about what God was doing in the world. But now because of Christ—dying that horrible death, shedding His blood—you who were once out of it altogether are in on everything. (Ephesians 2:11-13 MSG)

O Father, O Jesus, O Holy Spirit, O Triune God, what a wonderful plan You had from before creation and are working out perfectly at this moment!! We are so thankful that You have saved us and made us part of the family, without us earning anything! Now continually make us thankful for Your presence and for Your leading us as we go through this day and every day of our lives ahead. In Jesus Christ name Amen

So then you Gentiles are no longer strangers and aliens, but you are fellow citizens with the saints, are members of God's household, having been built on the foundation of the apostles and prophets, Christ Jesus himself being the cornerstone, (Ephesians 2:19-20 ESV)

THOUGHTS:

Speaking to Gentiles means God has shown that His plan from the beginning was not only to save the Jews, but to save everyone even us Gentiles. HALLELUJAH!

O Father, thank You for bringing us into the household of God. O Holy Spirit help us to grow in our understanding of the teachings of Bible and to have true faith in Jesus, Who holds the Family together. In the Powerful Name of the Cornerstone, Jesus Christ So Be It.

In Christ Jesus the whole household of God, being joined together, grows into a holy temple in the Lord. In him you also are being built together into a dwelling place for God by the Spirit. (Ephesians 2:21-22 ESV)

O Father, we have such a long way to grow to be holy and we need lots of continuing guidance through the Holy Spirit and lots of forgiveness! O Holy Spirit, we need Your help this day to live to please God and to grow in holiness. So, give us ears that hear Your guidance and hearts that obey! In Jesus Christ name So Be It.

LINDA MCGREGOR CLARK

I kneel before the Father and pray that he may grant you, according to the riches of his glory, to be strengthened with power in your inner being through his Spirit, and that Christ may dwell in your heart through faith... (Ephesians 3:14; 16-17a CSB)

O Father, thank You for the gift of Jesus Christ and for His Holy Spirit, Who lives in Your children to enable us to believe the Truth!! Strengthen us in our faith this day and make us aware of Your presence and Your working in our lives as Christ lives in our hearts. In Jesus Christ name So Be It.

Now to God who is able to do above and beyond all that we ask or think according to the power of the Holy Spirit who works in us— to God be glory in the church and in Christ Jesus to all generations, forever and ever. Amen. (Ephesians 3:20-21 CSB)

THOUGHTS:

A wonderful prayer of praise right out of the Bible! This enables us to praise our God by using His own words of Truth.

O Father make us children who praise You often! Fill us with deep love and thankfulness for Your workings in our lives! Thank You for the Holy Spirit, who is working in us, so we can glorify You. In Jesus Christ name Amen

I, a servant of the Lord, beg you to lead a life worthy of your calling, for you have been called by God. Always be humble and gentle. Be patient with each other, making allowance for each other's faults because of your love. (Ephesians 4:1-2 NLT)

O Father, thank You for calling us into Your family!! Now change us into the children You expect us to be, humble, gentle, patient and loving. We need lots of help from the Holy Spirit to develop into what You expect and we are so thankful that Jesus is praying for us continually and that You're always ready to forgive us and help us begin again. In Jesus Christ name Amen

LINDA MCGREGOR CLARK

Put away lying, speak the truth, each one to your neighbor, because we are members of one another. Be angry and do not sin. Do not let the sun go down on your anger, and don't give the devil an opportunity... you are to do honest work with your own hands, so that you have something to share with anyone in need. No foul language should come from your mouth, but only what is good for building up someone in need, so that it gives grace to those who hear. And do not grieve God's Holy Spirit. You were sealed by him for the day of redemption. (Ephesians 4:25-30 CSB)

THOUGHTS:

Words can be very hurtful, therefore we need to consider carefully if the words we are saying are true or gossip or helpful for the situation. Ask yourself if your words are necessary or if it would be better to hold your tongue. It is best to use our words to encourage others or to give someone grace.

O Father open our eyes to the times, show us that we are not living according to Your desires and cause us to really desire to live to please You. It is so easy to lie or carry a grudge and to hang on to anger, which gives the devil an opportunity to stir up trouble! Then there's foul language, O Father, we fail at that often and we live among people with foul mouths, HELP us to keep our mouths pure and to live to please You in all things. In Jesus Christ, our Savior's name Amen

Do not grieve the Holy Spirit of God, by whom you were sealed into God's Family for the day of redemption. Let all bitterness and wrath and anger and clamor and slander be put away from you, along with all vengefulness. Be kind to one another, tender-hearted, forgiving each other, just as God in Christ also has forgiven you. (Ephesians 4:30-32 NASB)

THOUGHTS:

We ourselves have been forgiven so many times by Jesus and He told Peter to forgive 70 times 70. Therefore we should be quick to show some mercy and forgivness to others who have offended or hurt us in some way. I would say we all need lots of forgiveness in this area too!

O Father we are so thankful for the Holy Spirit, Who has sealed us into the family of God because of Christ's sacrifice. We need lots of help to always live like You expect!

O Holy Spirit remind us often to be kind, tender hearted, and forgiving like You are. Our natural inclination is to be angry and want vengeance or hold a grudge. O Father forgive us and fill us with Your love so we won't grieve the Holy Spirit. In Jesus Christ name Amen

LINDA MCGREGOR CLARK

Be imitators of God, as beloved children. And walk in love, as Christ loved us and gave himself up for us, a fragrant offering and sacrifice to God. But sexual immorality and all impurity or covetousness must not even be named among you, as is proper among saints. (Ephesians 5:1-3 ESV)

O Holy Father, we live among people whose lives are full of sexuality, impurity, and covetousness, and it is very probable that we've easily picked up some of these sins. So, before we can be imitators of You, we need to repent! O Holy Spirit show us our sins and help us to change. O Jesus, thank You so much for Your blood that washes us clean and brings us forgiveness. Most gracious God help us to be good and kind and to reflect the sweet personality of Christ. In His precious name Amen

---

Obscene stories, foolish talk, and coarse jokes—these are not for you. Instead, let there be thankfulness to God. You can be sure that no immoral, impure, or greedy person will inherit the Kingdom of Christ and of God. For a greedy person is an idolater, worshiping the things of this world. (Ephesians 5:4-5 NLT)

O wow God, we are all guilty of doing these things and we need Your forgiveness! This world in which we live is obscene and we have gotten immune to it. Help us to recognize impurity, greed and lack of thankfulness in our own lives then to repent quickly. Thank You so much for constant grace and forgiveness through the sacrifice of the Cross of Christ Jesus. Thank You Holy Spirit for convicting us of our sin and for guiding us in God's way to live. Thank You Jesus that You are praying for us continually. Hallelujah Amen

Do not be fooled by those who try to excuse their sins, for the anger of God will fall on all who disobey him. Do not participate in the things these people do. For once you were full of darkness, but now you have light from the Lord. So, live as people of light! For this light within you produces only what is good and right and true. Carefully determine what pleases the Lord. (Ephesians 5:6-10 NLT)

O Father forgive us for taking sin lightly and help us to recognize our own sin then to immediately stop and repent. O Holy Spirit, help us to live as people of Light, producing goodness, righteousness and truth, which will please the Lord. In Jesus Christ name Amen

---

Be careful to learn what is pleasing to the Lord...and be careful how you walk, not as unwise men but as wise, making the most of your time, because the days are evil. So then do not be foolish but understand what the will of the Lord is. (Ephesians 5:10; 15-17NASB)

O Father help us to really understand what is pleasing to You and to walk in that way. O Holy Spirit fill us with wisdom from above and forgive us when we're foolish. In Jesus Christ name Amen

LINDA MCGREGOR CLARK

So, don't be foolish, but understand what the Lord's will is. And don't get drunk, which leads to reckless living, but be filled by the Holy Spirit:...giving thanks always for everything to God the Father in the name of our Lord Jesus Christ, submitting to one another in the fear of Christ. (Ephesians 5:17-18, 20-21 CSB)

O Father forgive us for turning to other things for comfort instead of You, things like alcohol or TV or eating or our phones. Forgive us for living recklessly and fill us with Your Holy Spirit to guide and comfort us. Help us to live thankful lives and to remember that You give us only what is best for us. In the Powerful Name of Jesus Christ Amen

Christ loved the church and gave himself for her to make her holy, cleansing her with the washing of water by the word. He did this to present the church to himself in splendor, without spot or wrinkle or anything like that, but holy and blameless.... This mystery is profound, but I am talking about Christ and the church. (Ephesians 5:25-27, 32 CSB)

O Father, we are so far from being holy and we need to repent!

O Jesus, thank You Thank You for making it possible to be forgiven and to one day be holy, when we get to heaven.

O but as we live here, we need the Holy Spirit to show us each time we are living in an unholy way, so we can repent. Give us ears to hear His correction and hearts to obey. In Jesus Christ name Amen

Honor YOUR FATHER AND MOTHER (which is the first commandment with a promise), SO THAT IT MAY BE WELL WITH YOU, AND THAT YOU MAY LIVE LONG ON THE EARTH.(Ephesians 6:1-3 NASB)

To honor means to treat someone with respect. To show kindness and love.

O Father, this is another hard requirement, because we are such sinners. Help us to understand what Honoring means. Give us kind and loving hearts and help us to be respectful, obedient and loving to our parents and to those in authority over us. According to Your word So Be It.

Not by way of eye service, as men-pleasers, but as slaves of Christ, do the will of God from the heart. With good will render service, as to the Lord, and not to men, knowing that whatever good thing each one does, this he will receive back from the Lord. (Ephesians 6:6-8 NASB)

O Father help us live our lives trying to please You by doing Your will. Forgive us when we go through our days without a thought about what You want us to be doing. Thank You for planning our lives and make us aware of Your plan then willing to obey. In Jesus Christ name Amen

LINDA MCGREGOR CLARK

A final word: Be strong in the Lord and in his mighty power. Put on all of God's armor so that you will be able to stand firm against all strategies of the devil....Stand your ground, putting on the belt of truth and the body armor of God's righteousness. For shoes, put on the peace that comes from the Good News so that you will be fully prepared. In addition to all of these, hold up the shield of faith to stop the fiery arrows of the devil. Put on salvation as your helmet, and take the sword of the Spirit, which is the word of God. Pray in the Spirit at all times and on every occasion. Stay alert and be persistent in your prayers for all believers everywhere. (Ephesians 6:10-11, 14-18 NLT)

Dear Father, thank You so much for equipping Your children with Your armor! Forgive us when we go out into our lives without it and try to live on our own. Fill us with Your Truth and Jesus's Righteousness. Also strengthen our faith, so we can use our faith to be strong and to shield us from bad thoughts. Fill us with Your Word, which is our protection from lies and remind us often to pray for ourselves and for each other. Help us want to stand firm and be good soldiers in Your army! In Jesus Christ name Amen

Peace be to the family of God, and love with faith, from God the Father and the Lord Jesus Christ. Grace be with all who love our Lord Jesus Christ with love incorruptible. (Ephesians 6:23-24 ESV)

O Father of Mercies, Giver of all graces, we thank You for giving us faith in Christ Jesus and drawing us with Your great love! Thank You for peace and for filling us with the Holy Spirit as our Teacher, Comforter and Guide. It's hard to practice what we believe, and He is our Helper. Give us ears to hear Him and hearts that are good soil which produce much fruit. In Jesus Christ name Amen

SAVED OR LOST?

❖

Oh, the joys of those who do not follow the advice of the wicked, or stand around with sinners, or join in with mockers. But they delight in the law of the Lord, meditating on it day and night. They are like trees planted along the riverbank, bearing fruit each season. Their leaves never wither, and they prosper in all they do. But not the wicked! They are like worthless chaff, scattered by the wind. They will be condemned at the time of judgment. Sinners will have no place among the godly. For the Lord watches over the path of the godly, but the path of the wicked leads to destruction. (Psalm 1:1-6 NLT)

SAVED:

1. Joyful in all things
2. Do not follow the advice of the wicked
3. Do not hang around with sinners
4. Do not join in with mockers
5. Delight in God's laws
6. Meditate on God's word day and night
7. Bear godly fruit
8. Watched over by God

LOST:

1. Wicked
2. Lifestyle of sin
3. Mock the things of God
4. Chaff: no roots, blown around by every new idea
5. Destructive

O Father, what an exact picture of the difference between Your children and the children of the devil. Open our eyes to recognize the differences and to make changes in our lives if we need to do so. I love the promise that You watch over the path of Your children! Help us to watch over our own actions, to be quick to repent and to live lives that are pleasing to You. Asking according to Your Word So Be It.

LINDA MCGREGOR CLARK

So now there is no condemnation for those who belong to Christ Jesus. And because you belong to him, the power of the life-giving Spirit has freed you from the power of sin that leads to death. The law of Moses was unable to save us because of the weakness of our sinful nature. So, God did what the law could not do. He sent his own Son in a body like the bodies we sinners have. And in that body God declared an end to sin's control over us by giving his Son as a sacrifice for our sins. He did this so that the just requirement of the law would be fully satisfied for us, who no longer follow our sinful nature but instead follow the Spirit. (Romans 8:1-4 NLT)

The law of Moses was unable to save us because of the weakness of our sinful nature. In Romans 3, Paul explains that the law's purpose is to keep people from having excuses, and to show that the entire world is guilty before God. For no one can ever be made right with God because the law simply shows us how sinful we are.

SAVED:

1. Belong to Christ Jesus, therefore we are not condemned
2. Holy Spirit has freed us from slavery to sin
3. No longer follow our sinful nature
4. Follow the Spirit

LOST:

1. Do not belong to Jesus, therefore under condemnation
2. Slaves to sin
3. Guilty before God
4. Follow the sinful nature

THOUGHTS;

For everyone who is Saved, these verses are a wonderful encouragement to grow in our obedience and to be so thankful for Jesus and the Holy Spirit.

For any who are Lost, these verses show you how to be saved: Believe that God sent His Son Jesus to be a human without sin and to pay the price of death for our sins on the cross and of course, to rise from the dead! Next Jesus gives the Holy Spirit to help the Saved follow Him.

Dear Father God thank You for Your perfect plan to make a way for us to be saved through faith in Jesus.
O Holy Spirit thank You for freeing us from slavery to sin, so we can follow You.
Jesus, please open the eyes of any lost and draw them into the family. Asking in Your name So Be It.

LINDA MCGREGOR CLARK

Those who are living according to the flesh set their minds on the things of the flesh [which gratify the body], but those who are living according to the Spirit, [set their minds on] the things of the Spirit [His will and purpose]. Now the mind of the flesh is death [both now and forever—because it pursues sin]; but the mind of the Spirit is life and peace [the spiritual well-being that comes from walking with God—both now and forever]; (Romans 8:5-6 AMP)

SAVED;

1. Live according to the Spirit
2. Set our minds on the will of the Spirit
3. Have a mind set on life and peace
4. Walk with God

LOST;

1. Live according to their flesh
2. Minds set on things that please their bodies
3. Have a mind of death that pursues sin

Dear Heavenly Father help us to understand on what our minds are set. Show us the need to focus on things that are pleasing to You and that to do so is hard work and takes much effort. We need diligence to protect our minds from the flesh and to pursue walking with You God now. Asking because of Jesus, may it be so.

For the sinful nature is always hostile to God. It never did obey God's laws, and it never will. That is why those who are still under the control of their sinful nature can never please God. But you are not controlled by your sinful nature. You are controlled by the Spirit if you have the Spirit of God living in you. (And remember that those who do not have the Spirit of Christ living in them do not belong to him at all.) (Romans 8:7-9 NLT)

SAVED:

1. Obedient to God's law
2. Controlled by the Spirit
3. Have the Spirit of God living in us
4. Live to please God
5. Belong to God

LOST:

1. Hostile to God
2. Do not obey God's laws
3. Cannot please God
4. Controlled by sinful nature
5. Do not have the Spirit of God living in them
6. Do not belong to God

O Father there are times when even Your children disobey but help us to recognize our sin and to turn back to following the Spirit. Thank You for freeing us from slavery to sin and keep us working to live lives of obedience that please You. Open the eyes of the Lost to truth and call them into the family. According to Your Word So Be It

LINDA MCGREGOR CLARK

For all who are led by the Spirit of God are children of God. So, you have not received a spirit that makes you fearful slaves. Instead, you received God's Spirit when he adopted you as his own children. Now we call him, "Abba, Father." For his Spirit joins with our spirit to affirm that we are God's children. (Romans 8:14-16 NLT)

SAVED:

1. Led by the Spirit of God
2. Children of God
3. Received God's Spirit when we were adopted
4. Call God Father
5. Know we are God's children because of the Spirit in us

Dear Holy Spirit give us ears to hear Your leading and willing hearts to be obedient children, who live pleasing lives before our Father God. Asking in Jesus Christ name So Be It.

For we know that all creation has been groaning as in the pains of childbirth right up to the present time. And we believers also groan, even though we have the Holy Spirit within us as a foretaste of future glory, for we long for our bodies to be released from sin and suffering. We, too, wait with eager hope for the day when God will give us our full rights as his adopted children, including the new bodies he has promised us. We were given this hope when we were saved. If we already have something, we do not need to hope for it. But if we look forward to something we do not yet have, we must wait patiently and confidently. (Romans 8:22-25 NLT)

SAVED:

1. Have the Holy Spirit to help us look forward to the transforming of our bodies at the Resurrection
2. Groan within ourselves as we await the redemption of our bodies
3. Are adopted children of God
4. Are saved by faith
5. Hope and eagerly await with patience the coming fulfillment of God's promises

Heavenly Father, in these words of Yours written by Paul in Romans there is much to learn, and we need understanding minds to comprehend the Truth. Thank You for our Teacher the Holy Spirit, who will help us and for Jesus, who prays for us every day. Thank You for every word in our Bibles, which are totally Your words! Fill us with the excitement of realizing that we can trust You to do exactly what You say. According to Your Word So Be It.

LINDA MCGREGOR CLARK

And the Holy Spirit helps us in our weakness. For example, we do not know what God wants us to pray for. But the Holy Spirit prays for us with groanings that cannot be expressed in words. And the Father who knows all hearts knows what the Spirit is saying, for the Spirit pleads for us believers in harmony with God's own will. (Romans 8:26-27 NLT)

SAVED:

1. Are weak in prayers
2. Holy Spirit helps us pray
3. Do not know what to pray
4. Holy Spirit prays for us
5. God the Father knows our hearts
6. Spirit prays according to God's will

O Holy Spirit, our Teacher, Comforter and Guide, thank You for helping us to pray according to the Father's will. It seems that this help is necessary any time we pray, since our prayers tend to be mostly about things we want, and we forget the need to repent and to be thankful. Continue Your work in our lives to make us more like Jesus. Praying in Jesus Christ name, Amen.

And we know that for those who love God all things work together for good, for those who are called according to his purpose. For those whom he foreknew he also predestined to be conformed to the image of his Son, in order that he might be the firstborn among many brothers. And those whom he predestined he also called, and those whom he called he also justified, and those whom he justified he also glorified. (Romans 8:28-30 ESV)

SAVED:

1. Love God
2. Everything that happens in our lives will work out for our good
3. Called according to God's purpose
4. Known before eternity
5. Predestined to become like Jesus
6. Are brothers and sisters of Jesus
7. Called into Salvation by faith
8. Justified, made right with God through faith in Jesus
9. Glorified, rewarded with heaven

O Father, what a wonderful blessing to have Your promise that everything You bring into our lives is for the purpose of making us better children and more like Jesus, our older Brother! It is hard to understand that You knew and chose us to be saved before creating anything. Thank You for calling us and giving us faith to believe in Jesus and for the promise of the final reward in heaven. From You and through You and to You are all things! To God be glory forever! Amen

What shall we say about such wonderful things as these? If God is for us, who can ever be against us? Since he did not spare even his own Son but gave him up for us all, won't he also give us everything else? (Romans 8:31-32 NLT)

SUCH WONDERFUL THINGS:

1. Everything that happens in our lives will work out for our good
2. Called according to God's purpose
3. Known before eternity
4. Predestined (determined in advance) to become like Jesus
5. Are brothers and sisters of Jesus
6. Called into Salvation by faith
7. Justified: made right with God through faith in Jesus
8. Glorified: rewarded with heaven

SAVED:

1. God is for us
2. God gave His Son up for us
3. God gives us everything we need for salvation

O Father as Your predestined, called, justified, glorified children, fill us with faith to trust You with all our needs because You are for Your children. According to Your Word So Be It.

Can anything ever separate us from Christ's love? Does it mean he no longer loves us if we have trouble or calamity, or are persecuted, or hungry, or destitute, or in danger, or threatened with death? No, despite all these things, overwhelming victory is ours through Christ, who loved us. And I am convinced that nothing can ever separate us from God's love. Neither death nor life, neither angels nor demons, neither our fears for today nor our worries about tomorrow—not even the powers of hell can separate us from God's love. No power in the sky above or in the earth below—indeed, nothing in all creation will ever be able to separate us from the love of God that is revealed in Christ Jesus our Lord. (Romans 8:35-39 NLT)

THOUGHTS:

WOW what a list of things that will "never, not ever" be able to separate us from the Love of God!! When we look carefully at this list, we realize there is "nothing, no nothing" that can or will be able to get between God's children, the Saved, and our Father God! Hallelujah, Hallelujah this brings out praise to our Father, our Savior and our Comforter!!

HOLY, HOLY, HOLY IS THE LORD GOD, THE ALMIGHTY, WHO WAS AND WHO IS AND WHO IS TO COME! Blessing and glory and wisdom and thanksgiving and honor and power and might, be to our God forever and ever. O Father thank You so much for such strong love on which we can totally depend! Thank You Jesus for paying our debt for sin and saving us, so we can have God's love! Thank You Holy Spirit for helping us understand even a little bit of God's love for His saved children! Hallelujah So Be It.

LINDA MCGREGOR CLARK

For I am not ashamed of the gospel, for it is the power of God for salvation to everyone who believes, to the Jew first and also to the Greek. For in it the righteousness of God is revealed from faith to faith; as it is written, "BUT THE RIGHTEOUS SHALL LIVE BY FAITH." (Romans 1:16-17 NASB)

SAVED:

1. Not ashamed of the gospel (the good news about Jesus)
2. Believe in Jesus
3. Righteous (do what is pleasing to God)
4. Live by faith

Dear Lord Jesus fill us with boldness to be proud that we are Christians and to live our lives by faith. Forgive us when we are silent, and we should speak out. Asking according to the Word, may it be so.

For ever since the world was created, people have seen the earth and sky. Through everything God made, they can clearly see his invisible qualities—his eternal power and divine nature. So, they have no excuse for not knowing God. Yes, they knew God, but they would not worship him as God or even give him thanks. And they began to think up foolish ideas of what God was like. As a result, their minds became dark and confused. Claiming to be wise, they instead became utter fools and exchanged the glory and majesty and excellence of the immortal God for an image [worthless idols] in the shape of mortal man and birds and four-footed animals and reptiles. (Romans 1:20-23 NLT)

LOST:

1. Clearly see God's eternal power and divine nature in creation
2. Have no excuse for not knowing God
3. Do not worship God
4. Are not thankful
5. Devise foolish ideas about God
6. Minds are dark and confused
7. Claim to be wise
8. Are utter fools
9. Worship worthless idols

O Father, these descriptions sure do describe our world in which we live! No one is righteous, no one seeks God, everyone's mouths are full of lies, cursing and bitterness, and there is no fear of God. O God, we need repentance! Please change our hearts to hearts full of the desire to live righteous lives, to live by faith and to never be ashamed of Jesus. So Be It.

LINDA MCGREGOR CLARK

We are made right with God by placing our faith in Jesus Christ. And this is true for everyone who believes, no matter who we are. For everyone has sinned; we all fall short of God's glorious standard. Yet God, in his grace, freely makes us right in his sight. He did this through Christ Jesus when he freed us from the penalty for our sins. For God presented Jesus as the sacrifice for sin. People are made right with God when they believe that Jesus sacrificed his life, shedding his blood. (Romans 3:22-25 NLT)

SAVED:

1. Made right with God by faith in Jesus Christ
2. All have sinned and fall short of God's standard
3. Made right in God's sight through His grace
4. Freed from the penalty of our sins by Jesus
5. Believe that Jesus sacrificed Himself by shedding His blood

Heavenly Father, when we read and see all this sin around us and even in us, we understand that ALL have sinned. But we are so thankful for Your decision to make a way for us to be forgiven and for our sins to be erased through the life, death, and resurrection of Jesus Christ! Give us repentant hearts, so we can live lives of faith. Praying in Jesus Christ name Amen.

God sent Jesus to demonstrate his righteousness, for he himself is fair and just, and he makes sinners right in his sight when they believe in Jesus. Can we boast, then, that we have done anything to be accepted by God? No, because our acquittal is not based on obeying the law. It is based on faith. So, we are made right with God through faith (in Jesus). (Romans 3:26-28 NLT)

THOUGHTS:

These verses are the Gospel and salvation is all by faith in who God is: righteous, fair and just, and what He's done: made sinners right in His sight by faith in Jesus.

O Father God, You are Righteous, Fair and Just and we are so thankful for the Gospel, the Good news about Jesus! Draw many more to faith in Jesus! Hallelujah, Hallelujah Amen

LINDA MCGREGOR CLARK

Therefore, since we have been made right in God's sight by faith, we have peace with God because of what Jesus Christ our Lord has done for us. Because of our faith, Christ has brought us into this place of undeserved privilege where we now stand, and we confidently and joyfully look forward to sharing God's glory. (Romans 5:1-2 NLT)

SAVED:

1. Made right in God's sight by faith
2. Have peace with God because of Jesus Christ
3. Jesus is our Lord
4. Have underserved privilege (grace)
5. Confidently and joyfully look forward to heaven with God

O Father, this is so Great what You have done for such undeserving sinners! We went from Your enemies to Your children by all Your doing and by our faith, the faith You have given us! Forgive us for living our lives in unthankfulness. Asking in Jesus Christ name So Be It.

And not only that, but we also boast in our afflictions, because we know that affliction produces endurance, endurance produces proven character, and proven character produces hope. This hope will not disappoint us, because God's love has been poured out in our hearts through the Holy Spirit who was given to us. For while we were still helpless, at the right time, Christ died for the ungodly. (Romans 5:3-6 CSB)

SAVED:

1. Know that suffering produces patient endurance
2. Endurance develops strong character
3. Strong character produces hope
4. Hope will never disappoint us
5. Have God's love filling our hearts
6. Have the Holy Spirit
7. Christ died for us when we were ungodly

O Father, suffering is hard, just like learning is hard, but the great results of spiritual growth to be had from suffering, when we turn to You for help, are good rewards. So please Holy Spirit give us hearts that want to learn and sharp minds to understand. Asking in Jesus Christ name So Be It.

LINDA MCGREGOR CLARK

But God clearly shows and proves His own love for us, by the fact that while we were still sinners, Christ died for us. For if while we were enemies we were reconciled to God through the death of His Son, it is much more certain, having been reconciled, that we will be saved [from the consequences of sin] by His life [that is, we will be saved because Christ lives today]. Not only that, but we also rejoice in God [rejoicing in His love and perfection] through our Lord Jesus Christ, through whom we have now received and enjoy our reconciliation [with God]. (Romans 5:8-11AMP)

SAVED:

1. Loved by God
2. Christ died for us while we were still sinners
3. Reconciled to God through Jesus death
4. Saved from the consequences of our sins by Jesus being alive today
5. Rejoice in God's love through Jesus
6. Jesus is our Lord
7. Through Jesus we enjoy being reconciled to God

O Father God, thank You for loving us even when we were still slaves to sin. Thank You Lord Jesus for reconciling us to God by Your death and for saving us from the terrible consequences of our sins by Your resurrection and life in Heaven. According to Your Word So Be It.

We know that our old life died with Christ on the cross so that our sinful selves would have no power over us, and we would not be slaves to sin. Anyone who has died is made free from sin's control. If we died with Christ, we know we will also live with him. In the same way, you should see yourselves as being dead to the power of sin and alive with God through Christ Jesus. (Romans 6:6-11 NCV)

SAVED:

1. Old sinful life died with Jesus on the cross
2. Sin has no power over us
3. No longer slaves to sin, but free from sin's control
4. Will live with Jesus
5. Dead to the power of sin
6. Alive to God through Jesus Christ

Thank You Jesus for rescuing us from slavery to sin and making us free to live lives that please God. Help us to be able to recognize when our old dead sinful selves try to lead us on the wrong path and then keep us on God's straight and narrow path of freedom from sin. Asking according to God's Word, may it be so.

So, do not let sin control your life here on earth so that you do what your sinful self wants to do. Do not offer the parts of your body to serve sin, as things to be used in doing evil. Instead, offer yourselves to God as people who have died and now live. Offer the parts of your body to God to be used in doing good. (Romans 6:12-13 NCV)

SAVED:

1. Do not let sin control our lives
2. Do not do what our sinful selves want to do
3. Offer ourselves to God for doing good
4. People who have died and now live

Dear Father, our sinful selves really want us to fall back into our old ways. Help us to fight back and to not let sin control us anymore. We are free to live lives that please You and that give us joy. Thank You so much for reconciling us to You through Jesus and setting us free from sin's control. Praying in Jesus name Amen

In the past you were slaves to sin, and goodness did not control you. You did evil things, and now you are ashamed of them. Those things only bring death. But now you are free from sin and have become slaves of God. This brings you a life that is only for God, and this gives you life forever. For the wages of sin is death, but the free gift of God is eternal life in Christ Jesus our Lord. (Romans 6:20-23 ICB)

SAVED:

1. Past were slaves to sin and could not live lives to please God
2. Now ashamed of evil things we did
3. Free from slavery to sin and now slaves to God
4. Live only for God
5. Will live forever
6. Receive the free gift of eternal life in Jesus Christ from God

LOST:
1. Slaves to sin
2. Cannot live lives pleasing to God
3. Earn the wages of sin, Death

Holy Father, who hates sin, we are so thankful that You rescued us from slavery to sin through the death and resurrection of Your Son Jesus! We pray for those who are lost and ask that You give them hearts to believe in Jesus, because He will rescue them from sin, when they repent, believe, and obey. So Be It.

So now there is no condemnation for those who belong to Christ Jesus. And because you belong to him, the power of the life-giving Spirit has freed you from the power of sin that leads to death...The Spirit of God, who raised Jesus from the dead, lives in you. And just as God raised Christ Jesus from the dead, he will give life to your mortal bodies by this same Spirit living within you. (Romans 8:1-11 NLT)

SAVED:

1. Are not condemned but belong to Christ Jesus
2. The Holy Spirit has freed us from the power of sin
3. The Spirit of God lives in us
4. Our bodies will be raised from the dead just like Jesus

Dear Father, what a blessing You have given to those who belong to Christ Jesus! We are forgiven for our sins and are no longer condemned. Thank You for the Holy Spirit living in us to teach and guide us to obedience by filling our hearts with love for You and for our neighbors. Finally, the promise that when Jesus comes back, we will have bodies just like Him, perfect and sinless! Thank You, thank You, thank You! According to Your Word So Be It.

For all who are led by the Spirit of God are children of God. So, you have not received a spirit that makes you fearful slaves. Instead, you received God's Spirit when he adopted you as his own children. Now we call him, "Abba, Father." For his Spirit joins with our spirit to affirm that we are God's children. (Romans 8:14-16 NLT)

SAVED:

1. Children of God
2. Led by the Spirit of God
3. Adopted as God's children
4. Can call Him Father
5. Holy Spirit affirms we are God's children

Hallelujah! Because of Jesus's sacrifice we, who believe, are children of God!! O Father thank You for adopting us and giving us the Holy Spirit to help us grow in loving You, living to please You and to be sure we are Your children. So thankful are we!! Amen

LINDA MCGREGOR CLARK

We know that in everything God works for the good of those who love him. They are the people he called because that was his plan. God knew them before he made the world, and he chose them to be like his Son so that Jesus would be the firstborn of many brothers and sisters. God planned for them to be like his Son; and those he planned to be like his Son, he also called; and those he called, he also made right with him; and those he made right, he also glorified. (Romans 8:28-30 NCV)

SAVED:

1. Called according to God's plan
2. Love God
3. Everything works for our good
4. God knew us before He created the world
5. Chose us to be like our older Brother Jesus
6. Called us
7. Made us righteous (right with Him)
8. Has glorified us

O Father, more fantastic promises for Your children, who You have known and chosen even before creation! Dear Father, we have a long, long way to go to become like Jesus! But thank You that You have, also, promised that You will not stop working in our lives to make us righteous through everything that comes into our lives. According to Your Word, so be it in our hearts.

What shall we say about such wonderful things as these? If God is for us, who can ever be against us? Since he did not spare even his own Son but gave him up for us all, won't he also give us everything else? Who dares accuse us whom God has chosen for his own? No one—for God himself has given us right standing with himself. Who then will condemn us? No one—for Christ Jesus died for us and was raised to life for us, and he is sitting in the place of honor at God's right hand, pleading for us. (Romans 8:31-34 NLT)

SOME OF THE WONDERFUL THINGS:

1. Called according to God's plan
2. Everything works for our good
3. God knew us before Creation
4. Chose us to become like Jesus
5. Made us righteous
6. Glorified us
7. Adopted as God's children
8. Led by the Spirit of God
9. Can call Almighty God Father
10. Under no condemnation

SAVED:

1. God is for us
2. God's own Son, Jesus, was given up for us all
3. Receive all we need from God
4. Chosen for God's own children
5. No one can accuse us or condemn us because God is for us
6. Jesus prays for us all the time

O Father this is a wonderful, special and long list! WOW, the Creator of All things, Who holds all things together, has made

LINDA MCGREGOR CLARK

us His adopted children, so we can call You Father! All we must do is believe that Jesus Christ has paid the price for our sins through His suffering, death and resurrection. Then we must repent of our many sins and begin to live lives pleasing to You Father God. Fill our minds and hearts with these truths. Asking in the name of Jesus, may it be so.

Can anything ever separate us from Christ's love? Does it mean he no longer loves us if we have trouble or calamity, or are persecuted, or hungry, or destitute, or in danger, or threatened with death? No, despite all these things, overwhelming victory is ours through Christ, who loved us. And I am convinced that nothing can ever separate us from God's love. Neither death nor life, neither angels nor demons, neither our fears for today nor our worries about tomorrow—not even the powers of hell can separate us from God's love. No power in the sky above or in the earth below—indeed, nothing in all creation will ever be able to separate us from the love of God that is revealed in Christ Jesus our Lord. (Romans 8:35-39 NLT)

List of things that cannot separate us from God:

1. Trouble
2. Calamity
3. Persecution
4. Hunger
5. Poor
6. In danger
7. Threatened with death
8. Nothing can ever separate us from God
9. Not death or life
10. Not angels or demons
11. Not our fears or worries
12. Not even Satan
13. Nothing in all creation

O my Father, You have said Nothing, Nothing, Nothing, Nothing can ever, at no time never separate us from Your Love! Thank You, Thank You so very much that we can be absolutely sure of Your love for us! Because of Jesus Christ our Lord we know the Love of our Father God. Hold us tight Father, because we have weak faith and we are so easily sidetracked from these wonderful things! Praying in Jesus Christ name Amen

LINDA MCGREGOR CLARK

If you confess with your mouth, "Jesus is Lord," and believe in your heart that God raised him from the dead, you will be saved. One believes with the heart, resulting in righteousness, and one confesses with the mouth, resulting in salvation. For the Scripture says, Everyone who believes on him will not be put to shame, For everyone who calls on the name of the Lord will be saved. (Romans 10:9-13 CSB)

SAVED:

1. Confess and acknowledge with our mouths that Jesus is Lord with full power and authority and majesty just as God
2. Believe in our hearts that God raised Jesus from the dead then we will be saved
3. Justified: made righteous, which means being free from the guilt of sin and being acceptable to God
4. Confirm our faith by speaking of our faith openly
5. Believe in Jesus, trust in Jesus, and rely on Jesus
6. Are never disappointed in our expectations about Jesus
7. Call on the name of the Lord Jesus to be SAVED

O Lord, You are our God; We will exalt You; We will praise Your name, for You have done wonderful things; plans formed of old, faithful, and sure. Thank You for the perfect plan to save us and for Jesus, Who carried it out! Fill our mouths with boldness to share our faith and to do the good duties which You have assigned to each of us. Calling on the name of Jesus, so be it.

Oh, the depth of the riches of the wisdom and knowledge of God! How unsearchable are his judgments and how inscrutable his ways! For who has known the mind of the Lord, or who has been his counselor? Or who has given a gift to him that God would need to repay it? For from him and through him and to him are all things. To him be glory forever. Amen. (Romans 11:33-36 ESV)

THOUGHTS:

Inscrutable means mysterious, unexplainable, perplexing; beyond our powers to know, understand or explain.

These are the verses to which I run when things are deeply troubling. They remind me that my Father God is All wise and has All knowledge. His judgements and His ways are way above my understanding and because He is my Loving Father, I can trust Him no matter what happens!

Then my prayer becomes:

FROM HIM AND THROUGH HIM AND TO HIM ARE ALL THINGS. TO HIM BE GLORY FOREVER. AMEN

Behold, God is our salvation and trust, do not be afraid; for the Lord God is our strength and song, and He has become our salvation. It is so, For FROM HIM AND THROUGH HIM AND TO HIM ARE ALL THINGS! TO HIM BE GLORY FOREVER! AMEN

LINDA MCGREGOR CLARK

Do not be conformed to this age, but be transformed by the renewing of your mind, so that you may discern what is the good, pleasing, and perfect will of God. (Romans 12:2 CSB)

SAVED:

1. Not conformed to the superficial values of the world
2. Transformed and growing spiritually
3. Renew our minds by focusing on godly values
4. Understand the good, acceptable, perfect plan and purpose of God for our lives

Blessed are You, O LORD, teach us Your statues! Open our eyes that we may see wonderful things in Your law. Make Your Word our delight and counselor. Make us understand the narrow way of Your precepts and incline our hearts toward Your Word. According to Your Word So Be It.

Your love must be real. Hate what is evil and hold on to what is good. Love each other like brothers and sisters. Give each other more honor than you want for yourselves. Do not be lazy but work hard, serving the Lord with all your heart. (Romans 12:9-11 NCV)

SAVED:

1. Have sincere, active love
2. Hate all ungodliness and do not tolerate wickedness
3. Hold tightly to what is good
4. Devoted to other Saved, just like family
5. Diligent in love and honor of others
6. Enthusiastically serve the Lord Jesus

Heavenly Father, the God of love, forgive us for not loving You with our whole hearts. Forgive us for not loving our neighbors as ourselves. Fill us with love for You and for each other, so we will be able to enthusiastically serve You and other Christians. Asking in Jesus Christ name Amen

LINDA MCGREGOR CLARK

Be happy with those who are happy, and weep with those who weep. Live in harmony with each other. Do not be too proud to enjoy the company of ordinary people. And do not think you know it all! Never pay back evil with more evil. Do things in such a way that everyone can see you are honorable. Do all that you can to live in peace with everyone. (Romans 12:15-18 NLT)

SAVED:

1. Share others' joy
2. Share others' grief
3. Live in peace with each other
4. Do not be conceited but associate with all
5. Do not overestimate yourself
6. Never take revenge
7. Be careful to do what is honorable
8. Do your best to live at peace with all

O God of our Lord Jesus Christ, Father of glory, thank You for giving us the Holy Spirit, Who gives us wisdom, understanding and greater knowledge of Jesus. We need help to live on this narrow path, which is described in Your Word. Thank You for bringing us, who once were far off, near by the blood of Jesus. Help us understand more and more the width, length, height, and depth of the love of Jesus and to be filled with the fullness of God. According to Your Word So Be It.

ENCOURAGEMENT AND COMFORT

Because of the pandemic in which we are involved, I believe we need encouragement and comfort from God's Word. Therefore, we will be looking at special scriptures in which God tells us not to fear, but to trust Him. Keep in mind that we have studied and learned that the Bible is the absolute perfect, unchanging, and trustworthy Word of God. So, every word in each scripture is True!

Truly my soul silently waits for God; From Him comes my salvation. He only is my rock and my salvation; He is my defense; I shall not be greatly moved. Trust in Him at all times, you people; Pour out your heart before Him; God is a refuge for us. Selah (Psalms 62:1-2 NKJV)

Dear Father God You are our salvation, our rock, and our defense. Fill our hearts with trust in You as our refuge especially during this pandemic and give us quiet souls as we wait for You to stop this sickness and the fear. In Jesus Christ name So Be It.

Yet I call this to mind, and therefore I have hope: Because of the Lord's faithful love we do not perish, for his mercies never end. They are new every morning; great is your faithfulness! (Lamentations 3:21-23 CSB)

HOPE that we have because of God's faithfulness, is sound Hope and Not just wishing hope that says, " Oh I sure hope so!" But this Hope is a positive knowing without a doubt that says, "I Know that God is faithful!"

O LORD in Your book were written, all the days ordained for each of us before we were even born. Please keep us thinking about Your faithful love and mercies that never end and fill us with hope(sure knowledge) in Your great faithfulness toward Your children. According to Your Word So Be It.

But I am poor and needy; Yet the LORD thinks upon me. You are my help and my deliverer. (Psalms 40:17 NKJV)

O LORD You know us personally, You think about us to help us and deliver us, the poor and needy people who have nothing to give to You. O our God, thank You, thank You for always helping us and for being our Deliverer. According to Your Word So Be It.

LINDA MCGREGOR CLARK

I will lift up my eyes to the mountains; From where shall my help come? My help comes from the LORD, Who made heaven and earth. He will not allow your foot to slip; He who keeps you will not slumber. (Psalms 121:1-3 NASB)

GOD:

1. Gives help to His people
2. Made heaven and earth
3. Will not allow His people to slip
4. Keeps His people
5. Never sleeps

Dear LORD, Who made heaven and earth, since You never sleep there is nothing that is out of Your control and You even protect us as we are sleeping. Help us to remember that our help always comes from You only. In Jesus Christ name So Be It.

Where can I go from Your Spirit? Or where can I flee from Your presence? If I ascend into heaven, You are there; If I make my bed in hell, behold, You are there. If I take the wings of the morning, And dwell in the uttermost parts of the sea, Even there Your hand shall lead me, And Your right hand shall hold me. If I say, "Surely the darkness shall fall on me," Even the night shall be light about me; Indeed, the darkness shall not hide from You, But the night shines as the day; The darkness and the light are both alike to You. (Psalms 139:7-12 NKJV)

THOUGHTS:

These verses have always been some of my favoite because they encourage me so much. It is such a wonderful thought that my Father God knows all about me and has complete control over my life, using every occurance to draw me closer to Him.

O Father what a wonderful message from these scriptures that there is absolutely no where we can go or anywhere we can be taken where You are not there! Also, even the darkest dark is like light to You. Therefore, if we are Your children and since the scriptures are Truth, then we can be sure nothing will happen to us without first being filtered through Your fingers. Give us trusting faith in this time and soothe our fears! According to Your Word So Be It.

LINDA MCGREGOR CLARK

Thus says the LORD, who created you, And He who formed you: "Fear not, for I have redeemed you; I have called you by your name; You are Mine. When you pass through the waters, I will be with you; And through the rivers, they shall not overflow you. When you walk through the fire, you shall not be burned, Nor shall the flame scorch you. For I am the LORD your God, The Holy One, your Savior. (Isaiah 43:1-3 NKJV)

THOUGHTS:

The Waters, the Rivers, the Fire each represent deepening troubles in our lives in which our LORD God is promising to be with His children, whom He knows so personally that He knows our names!!!

O Father the Holy One, our Savior, these verses are so encouraging to us in this terrible time of Covid-19. It feels like we are in the fire! Give us hearts that trust in Your promise in these words and take away our fear. Remind us throughout these days that You know us by name, we are Your children and You never leave or forsake us. According to Your Word So Be It.

I will say of the LORD, "He is my refuge and my fortress; My God, in Him I will trust." Surely He shall deliver you from the snare of the fowler And from the perilous pestilence. He shall cover you with His feathers, And under His wings you shall take refuge; His truth shall be your shield and buckler. (Psalms 91:2-4 NKJV)

THOUGHTS:

"Snare of the fowler" means hidden traps.

LORD: whenever you see Lord written in all uppercase letters it represents God's personal name YHWH "I AM," The Self-Existent One, Who never changes.

O LORD, our God and Father what an awesome picture of Your protection of us as a Mother bird protects her chicks under her feathers and wing. Help us to keep our minds focused on Your True words that tell us You are our refuge to run to! In Jesus Christ name may it be so.

LINDA MCGREGOR CLARK

Our God is in heaven. He does what he pleases. Family of God, trust the LORD; he is your helper and your protection. You who respect(fear)the LORD should trust him; he is your helper and your protection. The LORD remembers us and will bless us. He will bless the family of God. The LORD will bless those who respect(fear) him, from the smallest to the greatest. May you be blessed by the LORD, who made heaven and earth. (Psalms 115:3-15 NCV)

GOD:

1. Is in heaven
2. Does whatever He pleases
3. Is our Helper and Protection
4. Remembers us and blesses us
5. Made heaven and earth

GOD'S FAMILY:

1. Trusts the LORD
2. Fears the LORD (deeply in awe)
3. Blessed by the LORD
4. Protected by the LORD

Dear Father God in heaven, this is definitely a time in our lives when we need to know You well, so we will be able to trust You fully. Thank You for telling us over and over that You have control of everything and You protect Your children. It's amazing to read that the Creator of the universe remembers us and protects us. Give us faith in You according to Your Word Amen

Who in all of heaven can compare with the LORD? The highest angelic powers stand in awe of God. He is far more awesome than all who surround his throne. O LORD God of Heaven's Armies! You rule the oceans. You subdue their storm-tossed waves. The heavens are yours, and the earth is yours; you created it all. Righteousness and justice are the foundation of your throne. Unfailing love and truth walk before you as attendants. Praise the LORD forever! (Psalms 89:6-9,52 NLT)

O LORD You are Ruler over all, Righteousness and Justice are the foundation of Your throne! What an awesome reminder that You our Father are Sovereign LORD of ALL!! Therefore, we ask You to help our scientists and Doctors to find the cure for this virus. We ask for protection for all the First Responders and all Caretakers. Also, Father, we ask for wisdom and discernment for all our Leaders, cause them to do the right things. O LORD God, You are the most awesome, powerful Creator of all, and we praise You now and forever! In Jesus Christ Name, So Be It.

LINDA MCGREGOR CLARK

L<small>ORD</small>, you have searched me and known me. You know when I sit down and when I stand up; you understand my thoughts from far away. You observe my travels and my rest; you are aware of all my ways. Before a word is on my tongue, you know all about it, LORD. You have encircled me; you have placed your hand on me. This wondrous knowledge is beyond me. It is lofty; I am unable to reach it. (Psalms 139:1-6 CSB)

Our Sovereign Father in heaven, what wonderful truth we've just read, You know us more fully then we know ourselves and have Your hand on us even during this quarantine! Remind us often that You are the Creator, You are in complete control and are working everything for Your glory and for the good of Your children who love You. According to Your Word So Be It.

Lord, you have been our dwelling place in all generations. Before the mountains were brought forth, or ever you had formed the earth and the world, from everlasting to everlasting you are God. (Psalm 90:1-2 ESV)

I am the Alpha and the Omega, the first and the last, the beginning and the end." (Revelation 22:13 ESV)

Just two verses out of many that tell us our God is the Living One who has no limits and is not dependent on time. He is the Beginning and the End. "When the beginning began, He already was. When the end comes, He shall endure unchanged." (Dr. David Strain)

O Father give us ears to hear and hearts to understand even a little of the immensity of Who You are. Help us to trust everything You do as being for our good, because of who our Father is. Forgive us for fretting and worrying about what's going on in the world around us and remind us to focus on the things above. So Be It.

LINDA MCGREGOR CLARK

To whom then will you liken God? Or what likeness will you compare with Him? It is He who sits above the circle of the earth, And its inhabitants are like grasshoppers, Who stretches out the heavens like a curtain And spreads them out like a tent to dwell in. (Isaiah 40:18,22 NASB)

LORD here is an example of a man trying to describe You, One who is impossible to describe with our feeble words. Open our hearts to understand You better and to be in deep awe of You. We need to know You well, so we will trust Your ways, praise You properly and submit joyfully to You. According to Your Word So Be It.

I am at rest in God alone; my salvation comes from him. He alone is my rock and my salvation, my stronghold; I will never be shaken. (Psalms 62:1-2 CSB)

GOD:

1. Gives rest
2. Salvation comes from Him
3. Is my rock
4. Is my stronghold (defense, fortress)
5. Keeps His children from being shaken

Heavenly Father, we want rest in You! Fill us with faith in You and Your Word, so we can have the rest about which we are reading, because as Your children, we need to stand firm and not be shaken. Asking in Jesus Christ name So Be It.

I will bless the Lord who guides me; even at night my heart instructs me. I know the Lord is always with me. I will not be shaken, for he is right beside me. (Psalms 16:7-8 NLT)

GOD:

1. Guides us
2. Instructs us
3. Is always with us
4. Is right beside us

Heavenly Father incline our hearts to Your word, so we will believe what we read and not be shaken but stand firm. Thank You in these verses we see that You are always with Your children guiding and instructing. Give us ears to hear and hearts that obey. In Jesus Christ name Amen

The LORD is my strength and song, And He has become my salvation; This is my God, and I will praise Him; My father's God, and I will extol Him. (Exodus 15:2 NASB)

O Lord God, the Alpha and the Omega, our Father the LORD, You are our strength and song, our salvation! We praise Your Holy name that You even think about us! We are so grateful for Jesus and all He did to make it possible for us to be in heaven with You. Make us aware of Your presence as we go through our daily lives, so we will be obedient children who praise You properly. In Jesus Christ name Amen

LINDA MCGREGOR CLARK

The LORD of hosts has sworn saying, "Surely, just as I have intended so it has happened, and just as I have planned so it will stand, (Isaiah 14:24 NASB)

THOUGHTS:

Is not this wonderful! The LORD of Heaven's Armies, our Father, has planned everything and His plans cannot be stopped! They will Stand!

All Praise and Glory and Honor and Power be to You O LORD! May Your name be treated as Holy in all our thoughts and actions. It is so comforting to know that You have all things in complete control. Blessing and glory and wisdom and thanksgiving and honor and power and might, be to our God forever and ever. Amen.

Yours, O LORD, is the greatness and the power and the glory and the victory and the majesty, indeed everything that is in the heavens and the earth; Yours is the dominion, O LORD, and You exalt Yourself as head over all. Both riches and honor come from You, and You rule over all, and in Your hand is power and might; and it lies in Your hand to make great and to strengthen everyone. (1 Chronicles 29:11-12 NASB)

THOUGHTS:

Remember all uppercase letters in **LORD** are referring to God's personal name that He gave to Moses when Moses asked to whom he was talking at the burning bush. God's answer was I AM THAT I AM. Today we call God YHWH or Jehovah or LORD, all to say, The God Who never changes, His words never fail, He is the Self-Existent One.

O Father we are learning about Your Greatness, Glory, Power, and Majesty, about who You are! Give us minds that grab hold of this astonishing information and that understand, so we will be thrilled to know You, to trust and obey You and to worship You in the way You expect. According to Your Word So Be It.

LINDA MCGREGOR CLARK

Great is the LORD, and highly to be praised, And His greatness is [so vast and profound as to be] unsearchable [incomprehensible to man]. Your kingdom is an everlasting kingdom, And Your dominion endures throughout all generations. (Psalms 145:3 AMP)

LORD:

1. Great
2. Highly Praised
3. Greatness no one can understand
4. Kingdom is forever
5. Dominion is forever

Our Father in heaven May Your name be respected as Holy and all Greatness and power and Dominion be Yours in this world. Fill us with better understanding of You, so we can praise You rightly. Asking in Jesus Christ name Amen

He counts the number of the stars; He calls them all by name. Great is our Lord, and mighty in power; His understanding is infinite. (Psalms 147:4-5 NKJV)

THOUGHTS:

Have you ever been out in the country or on a high point, where there are no lights around and no clouds? Well, if you have and you looked up, you will see thousands of stars! So many you could not count them, but our God created them, counted them and named each one!

Heavenly Father, You are Great, have mighty power and have unlimited understanding! We are so thankful for our forgiveness and salvation through our faith in Jesus our Lord and Savior. We pray that some day soon all of us get a chance to see some of the many, many stars You have created to see just a small glimpse of Your Glory. May it be so.

LINDA MCGREGOR CLARK

But the LORD is the only true God. He is the living God and the everlasting King! The whole earth trembles at his anger. The nations cannot stand up to his wrath. But the LORD made the earth by his power, and he preserves it by his wisdom. With his own understanding he stretched out the heavens. When he speaks in the thunder, the heavens roar with rain. He causes the clouds to rise over the earth. He sends the lightning with the rain and releases the wind from his storehouses.
(Jeremiah 10:10-13 NLT)

LORD:

1. Only True God
2. The Living God
3. The Everlasting King
4. Whole earth trembles at His anger
5. Nations cannot stand against His wrath
6. Made the earth by His power
7. Preserves the earth by His wisdom
8. Created the heavens
9. Caused rain, lightning and wind

O LORD, our Father, such overwhelming information about You! It is awesome to realize that The Living God, the Only True God, the King of the universe takes notice of us and chose us to spend eternity with Him in heaven! Thank You Jesus for paying the terrible, awful price to wash away our sins. May we be repenting children who hate our sins. In Jesus Christ name Amen

Printed in the United States
By Bookmasters